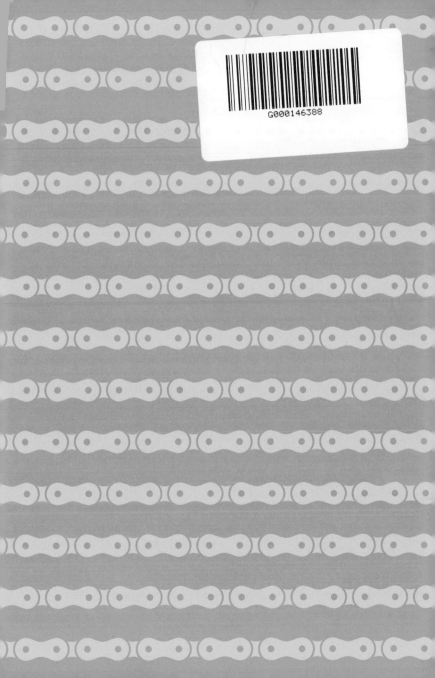

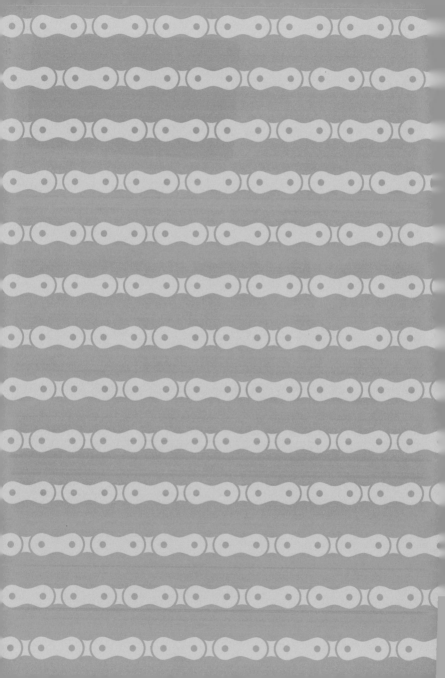

# RIDE

RIDE

An Hachette UK Company
www.hachette.co.uk

Summersdale Publishers Ltd
Part of Octopus Publishing Group Limited
Carmelite House
50 Victoria Embankment
LONDON
EC4Y 0DZ
UK

www.summersdale.com

Printed and bound in Poland

ISBN: 978-1-78685-260-1

Substantial discounts on bulk quantities of Summersdale books are available to corporations, professional associations and other organisations. For details contact general enquiries: telephone: +44 (0) 1243 771107 or email: enquiries@summersdale.com.

# RIDE

## A FACT-PACKED TOUR THROUGH THE WORLD OF CYCLING

## RAY HAMILTON

summersdale

# CONTENTS

## NOTE ON SOURCES

The websites I have come across during my research for this book are far too numerous to list, but I do recommend the first-class British Cycling website (www.britishcycling.org.uk), which I have used extensively to check facts and fill in gaps in my knowledge. It contains a wealth of information about how to get into whatever cycling you want to get into, as well as information about British riders and events across the entire competition range. If your cycling pursuits are purely leisurely, you should also check out the national cycling charity CTC's website (www.ctc.org.uk).

To the best of my knowledge, the facts and figures in this book are correct as at the end of October 2017.

# INTRODUCTION

*Bicycling is a healthy… pursuit, with much to recommend it, and, unlike other foolish crazes, it has not died out.*

The Daily Telegraph, 1877

This book is an update of the 2013 publication *The Joy of Cycling*. Since then, cycling has continued to go from strength to strength around the world, as a sport and as a leisure pursuit. New superstars like Chris Froome and Peter Sagan have emerged on the road and Mark Cavendish and Geraint Thomas have joined Froome on the exclusive list of British riders to have worn the yellow jersey in the Tour de France. On the track, Jason Kenny has matched Chris Hoy in winning a total of six Olympic gold medals, more than any other British athletes in history. Kenny also married Laura Trott, currently the most successful female track cyclist in Olympic history and Britain's most successful female Olympic competitor in any sport. If genetics have their way, their children may one day challenge them for the title of most successful British competitors of all time.

Cycling continues to have a lot going for it as a leisure pursuit, and none of that really changes from one year to the next. The ability to travel at around three times the pace of walking for the same amount of effort remains as attractive now to millions of adults and children across the globe as it was to the early riders of the 'boneshakers' and penny-farthings of the late nineteenth century. As more and more of us take to two wheels today, this edition of the book contains advice on how to look after our bikes and improve our cycling.

Cycling also has longevity going for it. Most bike riders start young and many will keep riding until well into their twilight years, whether to remain fit and healthy or just for the sheer fun of it. And there are those who could simply not imagine life without the more extreme forms of cycling – from professional racers to round-the-world tourers, or from daredevil mountain bikers to Guinness World Record seekers.

Bikes feature in many of our earliest memories. For me, it was trying to keep up with my older brother, Ken, as he pedalled effortlessly for miles over a ridiculous number of hills to the sand dunes of Irvine or the shores of Loch Lomond. There were times on those days when I found it difficult to remember what he looked like from the front.

And we never forget the first time a child of our own pedals away without stabilisers. At first oblivious to the fact we have let go of the saddle, then the inevitable wobble of panic as they realise we are no longer there, then the look of joy/relief/satisfaction on their little faces as they realise they are going to survive. With my daughter, Holly, it was more a look of grim determination. As a child who took her childhood very seriously, she went on to declare Halfords her favourite shop at the age of seven. She could have chosen Toys R Us, but she didn't. She chose a bike retailer. Sometimes it's hard not to be proud of them.

But no childhood memories of, or lifelong love affairs with, the bicycle would be possible if a volcano in the Dutch East Indies hadn't erupted in 1815. This book will justify that seemingly ridiculous claim before looking at the earliest incarnations of the bike. It will follow its evolution from a thing of wonder to a utilitarian form of transport and then on to the lean, mean racing machines that we marvel at during the Tour de France or the Olympics. It will look at the bike's survival in the face of monstrous levels of motorised transport and rejoice in its recent resurgence.

As the human race re-evaluates its position on planet earth, bikes are once more being seen as an integral part of the future, not the past. On account of their obvious ecological, financial and health advantages, they are once more part of the solution, not the problem. Many cities already bring joy to cyclists with city-centre rental schemes and safer cycle lanes and paths.

Like all subject matter of such historical, cultural and practical significance, cycling is awash with interesting characters and anecdotes, many of which this book takes a lighthearted look at. Read on to discover what led female Victorian cyclists to torture their cats and dogs, why Pope Pius XII refused to bless a pink jersey and why a sprint to the line in a 1,000-metre track race at the 1908 London Olympics never happened.

# CHAPTER 1

# *THE 'ERUPTION' OF THE BICYCLE*

*Progress should have stopped when man invented the bicycle.*

Elizabeth West, *Hovel in the Hills*

In 1815 the volcanic Mount Tambora in the Dutch East Indies erupted, and it forgot to stop. Within three months, it had filled the skies of the northern hemisphere with grey ash cloud, blocking out the sun and causing northern Europe and North America to be drenched in cold rain. The following year became known as 'the year without a summer'. Crops failed, including the oats needed to feed horses, so farmers and other horse owners had to shoot them rather than let them die of starvation.

It is thought that the resulting lack of horses inspired the German inventor Karl Drais to research new ways of horseless transportation, and led him in 1817 to invent the literally revolutionary all-wooden *Laufmaschine* (running machine), also known as the 'draisine' and the 'hobby horse'. There were no pedals but there were two wheels joined together and a means to steer them in a forward motion as your legs ran at a pace hitherto unknown to mankind. This was the ancestor of the modern bicycle and a definite step towards mechanised personal transport. Agriculture recovered, however, and Drais's idea was shelved for the next 40 years or so.

In the second half of the nineteenth century, though, trial and error spawned a bewildering array of contraptions that followed the basic form of Drais's running machine:

## BONESHAKER

With pedals now attached to the front wheel, the velocipede (literally, 'fast foot'), or boneshaker, invented in 1860s Paris did indeed shake the bones as riders traversed the cobblestones of the city. The pain was eased slightly with the later addition of metal 'tyres' to the wooden wheels, but not by much.

Only the rich could afford to own one outright, as they are said to have cost the equivalent of an average worker's pay over six months, and not that many people could afford to rent them by the minute even in the rinks that were set up for that purpose in Europe and America.

Not many boneshakers survive, as most of their metal frames and 'tyres' were melted down to help produce the armaments of World War One, and those that do survive command prices of several thousand pounds when they change hands.

## *PENNY-FARTHING*

This was a 'high-wheeler' made from metal in the 1870s and 1880s, and named 'penny-farthing' on account of its different-sized wheels. The rider sat on a saddle over the much larger front wheel, which was so designed in order to better absorb the shock of metal wheels on poorly paved surfaces. This front wheel was up to 1.5 metres (5 feet) in diameter, about double the size of today's bicycle wheels, while the smaller rear wheel was a mere 40 cm (16 in.) in diameter.

The penny-farthing became ridiculously popular, given how difficult and dangerous it was to ride. Problems with braking, steering or just being knocked sideways in a breeze all took their toll. Injury, and quite often death, awaited those who were suddenly rotated 180 degrees forward after applying the brakes. For obvious reasons, this became known as 'taking a header' and the penny-farthing came to be referred to as the 'widow-maker'.

When 'safety' bicycles (see 'Rover safety' below) were introduced in the mid 1880s, diehard penny-farthing riders would come to refer somewhat ironically to their bikes as 'ordinaries' in order to distinguish them from the newfangled contraptions with two similar-sized wheels.

### RE-CYCLED FACT

#### 'It's like riding a bike'

We may not easily forget how to ride a bike, but it's not always that easy to get the hang of it in the first place. Nowadays parents can teach their children the skill and balance required, but that wasn't the case for the early riders. It was such an unnatural thing for them to ride a velocipede, never mind a high-wheeler like the penny-farthing, that riding instruction books were published and riding academies, very much the equivalent of today's driving schools, sprang up on both sides of the Atlantic to satisfy the demand.

## HIGH-WHEEL TRICYCLE

While men rotated to death on their own front axles, many ladies who were confined to corsets and long skirts took to the parks on tricycles with two giant rear wheels and one smaller front one. These machines also afforded greater dignity to gentlemen such as doctors and clergymen, who could not be seen to be flying through the air by the members of Victorian society they served. Queen Victoria herself owned such a high-wheeled tricycle, a 'Royal Salvo', but there is no evidence that she rode it.

## HIGH-WHEEL SAFETY

The high-wheel safety was more of a 'farthing-penny' than a penny-farthing, as the rider-carrying large wheel was swapped to the back in an attempt to reduce the 'death by rotation' statistics – the smaller wheel at the front prevented the whole bike from rotating forwards when the brakes were applied.

## ROVER SAFETY

The British cycling industry started in Coventry and took a huge step forward with the introduction there of John Starley's 'Rover' in 1885. Now back to two wheels of similar height (so that both feet could be placed 'safely' on the ground), but with solid rubber tyres, a steerable front wheel and a chain drive to the rear wheel, the Rover was much faster than anything that had come before and a bit more comfortable. The riders of high-wheelers literally and metaphorically looked down on these new imposters, referring to them as 'dwarf machines', 'beetles' and 'crawlers'.

But it was during the development of Starley's safety bikes that the diamond-shaped frame that has survived to this day came to be recognised as the most efficient and effective design for the core of a bicycle; and the addition of pneumatic tyres in the 1890s was welcomed by backsides everywhere and continues to be appreciated (or, at least, taken for granted) by the posteriors of today.

---

### RE-CYCLED FACT

#### Air we go!

John Dunlop was a Scottish veterinary surgeon practising in Belfast in 1887 when he took it upon himself to develop the first practical pneumatic tyre to make his young son's tricycle more comfortable. Willie Hume, the captain of the Belfast Cruisers Cycling Club, proved the tyre's worth by winning races on it and commercial production began in 1890.

---

And so it was towards the end of the nineteenth century that the bicycle once more came to threaten the horse as the main form of human transport, but this time without the aid of volcanic eruption or crop failure. As Butch Cassidy (Paul Newman) declared after performing stunts on a safety bike to impress Etta Place (Katharine Ross) in *Butch Cassidy and the Sundance Kid*: 'The future's all yours, you lousy bicycle.'

Ironically, the bicycle industry itself would soon come under threat from its own products, as the mechanics and pneumatics it invented soon began to be applied to the early forms of the motor car. The Wright brothers would even have the audacity to apply the knowledge they gained repairing bikes to their rudimentary flying machines. And the riders of bikes didn't exactly help themselves either, demanding the improved riding surfaces that would literally pave the way for the motor car.

But the bike would survive and so, for the record, would the horse.

### RE-CYCLED FACT

#### The way ahead

It is a little-known fact that road surfaces were greatly improved in the late nineteenth century thanks to campaigns organised by pioneering cyclists and before the age of the motor car. Some raised cash themselves to help fund the much-needed repair of roads that were originally built to carry horse-drawn carriages, and some even experimented with different road surfaces. Granite, tarless macadam, rubber and hardwoods were all trialled before the more permanent solution of tarmacadam came along. Mostly, though, the cycling associations that were springing up around the country brought about improvements by taking parish councils to court to force them to maintain their roads to the standard demanded by the Highway Act of 1835. They enlisted the help of well-connected members of cycling clubs to exert pressure on councils. These well-connected people included Sir Alfred Frederick Bird, proprietor of the famous Bird's food business and also a champion tricyclist.

# CHAPTER 2

# *THE EVOLUTION OF REVOLUTION*

*Other forms of transport grow daily more nightmarish.
Only the bicycle remains pure in heart.*

Iris Murdoch, *The Red and the Green*

It is fair to say that the bicycle has been life-changing for many people, and for many different reasons. In this chapter, we will look at its usage and development in the context of the role it has played (primarily in Britain) in the pursuit of everything from leisure and business to war and the emancipation of women.

## *CULTURAL CHANGE*

For those who could afford them in the late nineteenth and early twentieth centuries, bicycles suddenly enabled day trips or even whole weekends away. Hitherto unexplored countryside was explored; as yet unseen seasides were seen. For many women, bicycles also meant an end to total reliance on men for transport.

Bicycle trips educated people about the geography and ways of life that existed beyond their natural doorsteps. City boys and girls met country boys and girls, and within a generation the gene pools of an area were extended as far as it was possible to cycle in a weekend. There may even have been some cross-fertilisation across the class divide as social barriers are said to have largely fallen away on bike rides, even if those barriers went straight back up on a Monday morning back in the real world.

The unprecedented social change of the time was personified in a remarkable 16-year-old girl called Tessie Reynolds, who, in 1893, took it into her head to cycle all the way from her home in Brighton to London Bridge and back in a day. This didn't just show that a young woman could be a supreme athlete, it showed that she didn't have to live her whole life in the town or village or street in which she was born.

Clothing was an immediate issue for female bike riders, it being apparent from the start that bicycle pedals could not be operated from the 'ladylike' side-saddle position then employed on a horse. Corsets and petticoats had to stay in the wardrobe if women were to enjoy the freedom and equality promised by the bicycle. Tailors got rich quick by providing the bloomers, knickerbockers and divided skirts that allowed women to mingle unchaperoned with their male counterparts on bicycle rides and to join in unisex games like bicycle polo. At a more utilitarian level, some women would even find the bicycle an indispensable means of carrying out their jobs, particularly those, such as midwifery, that involved getting from house to house over a wide catchment area.

In spite of such heady beginnings for the fairer sex, however, cycling remained largely a male pastime. Initially, this had much to do with the costs involved, and with the fact that the predominantly male family breadwinner had more need for transport than those left at home.

## RE-CYCLED FACT

### The lunacy of cycling

As the bicycle became safer to ride and more widely available, some members of Victorian society railed against what they saw as an unnecessarily dangerous pastime. In 1894, a report by the Commissioners in Lunacy pointed out an increase in the numbers of 'idiots and lunatics' in England and Wales and partially attributed the increase to bicycle riding, pointing out that the circular motion of the wheels caused the human brain to reason in circles, which in turn led to a weakening of the mind.

The media on both sides of the Atlantic, including *The New York Times*, were quick to pick up on this development, with reports of 'otherwise mild clergymen and physicians' mowing down pedestrians and leaving them for dead at the side of the road. Women bicycle riders were said to be rendering themselves infertile and many were reported, as a direct result of the circular motion of their bicycle wheels, to have taken to torturing their domestic pets 'in the most frightful fashion'.

## ON THE JOB

In addition to the midwifery already mentioned, other professions that were to make extensive use of the bike included the following:

### Police officer

The great British 'bobby' must have been pleased to give his 'plates of meat' (that's 'feet' for anyone unfamiliar with Cockney rhyming slang) a well-earned rest upon the advent of the bicycle, and must initially have felt greatly empowered to be on a form of transport quicker than the foot. (Although I do accept that the odd criminal might have escaped over the fields on horseback, I doubt it would have been a very common occurrence.)

Taking a lead from the USA and Canada over a hundred years later, a twenty-first-century revival is seeing mobile police officers on state-of-the-art mountain bikes in many cities and rural areas around the world, including across Britain. Advantages are considered to be faster response times compared with police officers on foot or police cars stuck in traffic; rapid access to incidents in places like housing estates, playing fields or canal towpaths; and greater connection with the younger generation.

### Soldier

As early as the Second Boer War (1899–1902) in South Africa, scouts and messengers used bikes, and cycle-mounted infantry conducted raids on both sides. An army cycling manual of the time recommended that riders should turn their bikes upside down and spin the wheels in order to spook enemy cavalry horses.

In World War One, the Germans had cycling companies within each of their 80 infantry battalions and the British Army had an entire Cyclist Division. In 1937, Japan included around 50,000 bicycle troops when it invaded China. In World War Two, BSA Airborne folding bicycles were sometimes parachuted in with the Allied paratroopers who used them to make a quick getaway as soon as they were on the ground behind enemy lines.

## Delivery rider

The jolly image of the British postman delivering letters on his trusty bike emerged with the penny-farthing of the late nineteenth century, and a quarter of Britain's letters were still being delivered on tens of thousands of 'Pashley Red' Post Office bicycles as late as the 1970s.

Private companies across the globe, including DHL for the final stage of some of their worldwide deliveries, still use the bicycle for delivering letters, packages and important documents. The takeaway food industry also plays its part in keeping the planet green, not least in the delivery of the ubiquitous pizza and in the iconic ice-cream-vending trolley bike. For true cycle-delivery chic, though, we need look no further than Amsterdam to see everything from flowers to furniture being delivered in bicycle baskets and trailers.

## RE-CYCLED FACT

### The self-riding bicycle

The self-driving technology being applied to cars has been introduced to bicycles in Amsterdam. The on-board computers take account of traffic and weather conditions to deliver the bikes safely to their riders in any part of the city, or to allow their riders to get on with other things while the bikes beneath them do all the work. Business people can make telephone calls or catch up on emails on their laptops en route to the office. Small schoolchildren can finish off their homework, no matter how bad the city-centre traffic becomes and without the need for their parents to accompany them on the journey to school.

Note: The self-riding bicycle is only available for sale on the first day of April each year.

## Butcher's boy

This black classic roadster was designed to carry heavy loads in the large wicker basket over the front wheel, and had a large metal plate hanging from the crossbar to advertise the company colours and logo. Like the Post Office bikes, these 'Delibikes', as they are now known, were mainly made by the Pashley bicycle company that started up in 1926 and is still going strong today.

### RE-CYCLED FACT
#### That Hovis ad on the telly

The 'butcher's boy' bike was equally useful for the delivery of bread, as evidenced by the iconic 1973 Hovis ad that forever implanted the theme from Dvořák's *New World Symphony* into British consciousness. The nation sighed nostalgically as 'Boy on Bike' delivered bread to old Ma Peggity at the top of Gold Hill in Shaftesbury, Dorset, before freewheeling back down to enjoy his own Hovis 'doorsteps' when he got home. The ad was directed by none other than future *Alien*, *Blade Runner* and *Gladiator* director, Ridley Scott.

### Factory worker

Memories of factory workers pouring through the gates en masse on their bikes were revived in the 2010 British film *Made in Dagenham*, which portrayed the struggle of women in 1960s Britain to get the same pay rates as male workers involved in the production of cars. Commuting to work by bike remains hugely popular in towns and cities around the world, and even in pockets of Britain.

Heavy, load-bearing bicycles also continue to be used as transport within large factories and warehouses where motorised vehicles are prohibited for safety reasons.

### Bicycle taxi

Until recent times we could only have the bicycle taxi experience when travelling in the rickshaws of Asia, but nowadays many major Western cities have students and others performing the same job in order to give tourists a fun, relaxing and environmentally friendly tour of their major sights.

## THE MOTORISED ENEMY

As soon as Henry Ford launched his Model T car, otherwise known as the 'Tin Lizzie', in 1908, bikes stopped being man's newest toy, but for another half a century the bike would remain the only toy that most people could afford. As the economic effects of World War Two finally began to wear off in the 1950s and 1960s, more people took to the roads in mechanised forms of transport and the bike was increasingly looked upon as the poor man's car, or the young person's plaything. In some cases, manufacturers even stopped worrying about whether bikes worked. The Raleigh Chopper of the 1970s and its smaller version, the Tomahawk, looked great, but they felt like they were designed for circus clowns to ride round and round on in the big top. However much you wanted to, it was very difficult to run away from home on a bike with an 'ape-hanger' handlebar, different-sized wheels and a spongy saddle the size of a small sofa.

As money was ploughed into car manufacturing (Peugeot, Opel, Morris, Rover, Hillman and Humber are just some of the bike manufacturers that converted to car-making) and the road infrastructure needed to support it, cycling became increasingly difficult and dangerous. As we will see, it would be the end of the twentieth century before politicians and planners started to address the folly of the decisions that their predecessors had taken, in terms of the environment and in terms of the health and well-being of the world's citizens.

Cycling remained more popular in western mainland Europe than in other developed countries in the twentieth century, primarily because road racing was a huge sport in countries like France, Italy and Spain. Roads were less crowded in parts of those countries than in Britain, particularly in the mountains where much of the racing took place.

Cycling also remained popular in areas like South East Asia and China, where the gulf between the rich and poor encouraged parallel economies – a motorised economy for the rich and a bicycle/rickshaw economy for the poor. As the poor outnumbered the rich, so bicycles continued to outnumber cars in the Far East long after cars had started to force bikes off the roads of western Europe.

In the USA, off-road cycling and bikes remained especially popular throughout the twentieth century. Initially, this was down to the popularity of track cycling as a spectator sport. Almost every major city had a velodrome in the first half of the twentieth century. The annual races at Madison Square Garden were as popular as baseball and gave rise to the Madison track cycling event that continues to this day. Track cycling did eventually fall behind baseball and American football in the national psyche by the middle of the century, but it would later be replaced by the mountain-bike and BMX crazes that swept the nation from the 1970s onwards.

# A BIKE FOR EVERYONE

Bicycles have evolved in different shapes and sizes, and using different technologies and materials, in order to meet the demands of a wide range of bike riders across the world.

## Mountain bike

Robust and great for off-roading, the mountain bike is ideal for the cross-country enthusiast who prefers woodland mud, rocky paths, tricky climbs and death-defying technical descents.

It was pioneered in 1970s America by the likes of Joe Breeze, Gary Fisher, Charlie Kelly and Tom Ritchey, and was a bit of a cross between a road bike and a BMX. It had heavier tubing than a road bike, and a wider fork to accommodate a wider tyre and bouncier suspension. Gary Fisher's name in particular became synonymous with the mountain bike, but the two first mass-produced models were the magnificently named Specialized Stumpjumper and the Univega Alpina Pro.

The bike industry was initially unimpressed by the upstart mountain-biking fraternity, but the latter's passion developed into, and very much remains, a mainstream activity across the globe.

## BMX

Strong but light frames and smooth tyres make these the ideal bikes for practising tricks on. Perfect your hops and grinds, and your 180s and 360s, before progressing to BMX racing, which became an Olympic sport at Beijing in 2008.

BMX is short for 'bicycle motocross', and the bikes were in fact designed in 1970s California in order to replicate the thrills and spills of motocross for youngsters. Chopper-style bikes, like the Schwinn Sting-Ray, were the obvious choice for BMX racing at the time, and the basic design that remains today stemmed from that style. Other bikes styled on the chopper motorbikes rendered iconic by the 1969 American road movie *Easy Rider*, and customised for BMX racing in the 1970s, included the then ubiquitous Raleigh Chopper and Tomahawk, also referred to as 'wheelies' (most of the weight was on the back, so doing a 'wheelie' was easy), 'high-risers' (on account of the 'ape-hanger' handlebar) and 'banana bikes' (on account of the curved saddle).

Notwithstanding the lack of grip on the smooth tyres of a BMX bike, brakes are not considered necessary – apparently that's what feet are for.

## Racing

Light and fast for those who take their road cycling seriously, racing bikes are ideal for long-distance commuting, club cycling and, of course, professional road racing. Variations include triathlon and time-trial (TT) bikes, with the former designed to keep the rider more forward and upright in the saddle in order to save the quadriceps for the running stage that follows the bike ride, and the latter made as streamlined as possible to reduce aerodynamic drag.

The early single-gear steel monsters ridden by the European road racers of the late nineteenth century have continually evolved into today's super-lightweight carbon-fibre machines incorporating state-of-the-art aerodynamics and electronic componentry. Even individual components have somehow managed to become cool. Imagine what the nineteenth-century men of steel would have made of an electronic groupset (the drivetrain of cogs and levers and cables without which a modern racing bike will go nowhere), a Fizik Arione Classic saddle made of carbon-reinforced nylon Wingflex and thermowelded Microtex, or a Speedplay Nanogram Zero Ti pedal.

## Hybrid

A hybrid is lighter than a mountain bike but sturdier than a racer, so is a great crossover option for cycling around towns and cities and into the surrounding countryside. It will also cope with 'mild' off-roading.

Size and riding position are influenced by the mountain bike (for example, a hybrid has a flat handlebar), but the smoother tyres are akin to those of racing bikes and make for better rolling on paved, or at least smooth, surfaces. Many manufacturers produce different variations on the hybrid theme, and you will see them advertised also as 'town and city', 'comfort', 'multi-use', 'lifestyle', 'commute', 'urban', 'fitness' and whatever else takes the marketing department's fancy. They are often designed with facilities like luggage racks and clothes-protecting mudguards and enclosed chain guards.

It is difficult to say when the first hybrids were introduced to the market as they have largely evolved from existing bike designs over the past two or three decades. The mass manufacturers today include Specialized and Giant.

## Touring

This bike does what it says on the tin, designed for comfort over long distances but with sufficient strength and mounting points to carry heavy luggage. The tandem is a romantic variation if you manage not to fall out for the entire trip.

It often looks like a normal racing bike from a distance (especially those with a dropped handlebar), but closer inspection will reveal a longer-than-usual wheelbase, heavy-duty wheels and the required luggage-mounting points. Touring bikes have been around for as long as people have wanted to tour on bikes, which is a long time. Distance is generally not an object, but if you want to cycle round the world on sometimes-difficult surfaces and/or in sometimes-extreme weather, you would do well to take the advice of specialists to determine just how industrial you need your touring or trekking bike to be. Significant touring-bike manufacturers today include Raleigh, Ridgeback and Dawes.

## Track

Track bikes are minimalist affairs, designed for speed in a velodrome and nothing else. There are no brakes, no gears and no freewheel – if the back wheel is turning, so are the pedals.

These bikes resemble stripped-down road-racing bikes, and there's not much point in buying one if you don't want to race competitively in a wooden velodrome. There are no hills to negotiate and there is no need to stop or slow down suddenly in a velodrome, hence the absence of gears and brakes.

## Roadster

The roadster is a classic utility bicycle once popular worldwide, not least because Raleigh and BSA exported them throughout the British Empire for as long as that empire held strong. They are still common in Africa, Asia, Denmark and the Netherlands.

A heavy steel but extremely reliable bike, the roadster is easily identifiable by its large wheels and a high 'sit-up-and-beg' handlebar. Once ubiquitous in Amsterdam and Beijing, it is still mass-produced in Asia, primarily for the sub-Saharan African market. A top-end range is still produced by Pashley Cycles, the British company that produced them for the postal workers, police officers and butcher boys of yesteryear.

## Folding

A normally small-wheeled utilitarian option, the folding bike saves storage space at home or in the office and can be taken on most forms of public transport. Just don't expect much speed from the small-wheeled versions.

Although the folding bicycle is particularly useful nowadays for commuters, it was originally designed to be used by infantry soldiers in the late nineteenth century. The Pedersen folding bicycle was used by the British Army in the Second Boer War, so infantrymen could fold them up and carry them on their backs across terrain that was not suitable for cycling.

Top manufacturers of folding bikes nowadays include Ridgeway, Dahon and Brompton.

## Recumbent

This bike places the rider in a laid-back reclining position, with body weight distributed more evenly, and therefore more comfortably, than on a conventional bike. This can be particularly useful for riders with chronic back or neck problems.

Other advantages of the recumbent include increased peripheral vision (because the head is not bent forward), less distance to fall in the event of an accident and improved aerodynamics (a recumbent holds the world speed record for a bicycle). Although it is one of the few types of bike not to adhere to the basic diamond-shaped frame that has been used since the late nineteenth century, and although people continue to stop and stare at one as if it had just arrived from outer space, the recumbent has in fact also been around since the nineteenth century, having evolved from the early stages of experimental design.

Recumbents are available as bicycles or tricycles (main manufacturers include Optima and Lightning), and as static exercise bikes.

## Electric

Also known as an e-bike, you pedal and use the gears as normal but a battery-driven electric motor will do the hard work for you. This is a more expensive option, but great value for money if you use it as an affordable alternative method of mechanised transport (no licence, MOT, motor insurance or petrol needed). It is also ideal for family biking holidays, even in mountainous terrain, if you have passengers in the form of small children to haul up those steep inclines. In later life, an e-bike will also keep you cycling beyond your natural capacity and enable you to keep up with younger family members or friends.

# CHAPTER 3

# CYCLING AROUND TOWNS AND CITIES

*You always know when you're going to arrive by bike.*
*If you go by car, you don't.*

Alan Bennett, British author and playwright

A lot of exciting things are happening nowadays for the benefit of the world's urban cycling fraternity. From large-scale urban redevelopment to idyllic rural and waterside cycle paths, planners and developers around the globe are responding to the growing demand for a better, safer cycling infrastructure. The benefits are obvious: healthier living, cleaner environments and more affordable transport.

At the turn of the twenty-first century many politicians and urban planners seemed to wake up to the stupidity of their predecessors, and reports of common sense have been flooding in from around the world ever since.

## UK TOWNS AND CITIES

Some UK towns and cities would sit better in the Netherlands or Denmark when it comes to cycling take-up. Around 25 per cent of journeys in Oxford and around 35 per cent of journeys in Cambridge are made on bikes, which is not far off the national averages of Britain's northern European neighbours.

Of course, university towns have always been way more cycle-friendly than larger urban sprawls, not least because many students can only afford bikes. And because these towns already had a cycling infrastructure of sorts (albeit one that had existed for centuries in some cases), they were better equipped to survive the short-sighted movement in the second half of the twentieth century to plan for ever-increasing traffic at the expense of cycling and the environment generally.

A number of investment schemes have been launched in the UK to fund safety measures and infrastructure changes in order to encourage more people to cycle more often. The schemes include schools-based and business-based education about the benefits of cycling, and 'bikeability' training for children and 'rusty' adults.

Bristol was awarded the status of 'Cycling City' when it launched the UK's first on-street bike-rental scheme in 2008, based on an existing Paris model. London continues to introduce and develop cycle superhighways to aid commuting in and out of the city; safe bike zones that offer traffic-free school runs; and its own bike-rental scheme.

Other cities with a growing take-up in cycling include Edinburgh, Exeter, Leeds, Leicester, Manchester, Norwich and York.

---

### RE-CYCLED FACT
#### Tour de Yorkshire

Yorkshire in particular has seen exponential growth in cycling activity since the first two stages of the Tour de France were staged there in 2014 and attracted millions of spectators to the city streets, rural roads and mountain climbs of the route. The Tour's organisers were equally ecstatic about the scenery offered up by the Yorkshire Dales. Dubbed the 'Tour de Yorkshire' at the time, an annual three-day cycling race of that name was initiated in 2015 and subsequently upgraded to a four-day race from 2018.

---

# AROUND THE WORLD

Elsewhere in the world, there are also some encouraging steps being taken to promote more cycling, although I'm going to have to make an exception when it comes to Beijing.

### Amsterdam, the Netherlands

Amsterdam is one of the places you would expect things to be happening on bikes, of course. Without over half a million bicycles in its concentrated city centre, Amsterdam would not be Amsterdam. It's a cultural thing as much as anything else, and it's a known fact that all Amsterdammers were in fact born on their bikes.

With almost 500 km (310 miles) of cycle paths, more and more roads being closed to traffic and car parking charges becoming increasingly exorbitant, it is estimated that over 60 per cent of all journeys in the inner city are now made by bike. The classic sturdy Dutch roadsters still in common use throughout the city are the *opafiet* ('grandpa's bike') and *omafiet* ('grandma's bike'). In common with their nineteenth-century ancestors, many of them have no brakes, so you have to pedal backwards to slow down or stop.

### Portland, Oregon, USA

Portland (population approx. 600,000) has achieved a 10 per cent cycling commuter rate by creating over 260 miles (420 km) of cycle paths to connect its many urban neighbourhoods, and by offering low-cost bicycles (complete with helmet, pump, lock, maps and rain gear) to its less wealthy residents. This take-up rate may not seem high when compared to, say, Amsterdam, but it is more than ten times the American national average and a staggering achievement in the otherwise car-centric Pacific Northwest region. Some companies even reward employees who cycle to work with vouchers that can be spent in the staff canteen.

The city added a bike share scheme in 2016, with an immediate take-up of around 50,000 rides per month.

### Beijing, China

There are nine million bicycles in Beijing, as singer-songwriter Katie Melua reminded us in her top-five UK hit of 2005. It is a sad fact, however, that the 'improved' road infrastructure put in place for the 2008 Beijing Olympics brought with it a huge increase in road traffic and made cycling more difficult and more dangerous. City planners now claim to be clawing back the previous position by restoring cycle lanes and introducing bike schemes, but they have a real mountain to climb.

The nine million bikes in question are mostly the roadsters that have been dubbed 'Flying Pigeons', which the revolutionary People's Republic of China decreed to be the approved form of transport for the masses in 1950. This heavy bike, which came in black or black, was considered to be one of three must-haves for each and every citizen, the others being a sewing machine and a watch. It was the perfect symbol of the egalitarian social system of the time – the promise of little comfort but a reliable ride through life. The Chinese government estimates that there are over half a billion Flying Pigeons around China today, many of them handed down from generation to generation.

## RE-CYCLED FACT

### Black Mambas

The Chinese industrial invasion of sub-Saharan Africa in recent decades has included the supply of a great many Flying Pigeons to Kenya, where they have been re-dubbed 'Black Mambas'. Many have an additional pillion (or passenger) saddle over the back wheel to allow their use as *boda-bodas* (taxis), and it is not unusual to see a Kenyan mother side-saddling on this two-wheel taxi holding onto two or three children.

## Copenhagen, Denmark

More than 60 per cent of Copenhageners commute to work or education by bike, making use of around 1,000 km (620 miles) of cycle lanes in the Greater Copenhagen area. It is possible to cycle to Roskilde, 30 km (19 miles) west of the city, and never leave a bike lane. Cyclists even have their own traffic lights, which let them go before cars.

The bike is like a fifth limb to the residents of Copenhagen, where cycling is a way of life, as opposed to some sort of subculture, which is how it is still viewed by many people in Britain and America. Danish journalist Mikael Colville-Andersen coined the term 'cycle chic' to describe just how fashionable and comfortable Copenhageners look riding their bikes in everyday clothing, and described the city's bike culture as follows: 'Copenhageners cycle to live, but they don't live to cycle.'

Copenhagen City Bikes, launched in 1995, was the first organised, large-scale, urban bike-sharing scheme in the world and has served as a model for the many self-service systems with fixed stands and specially designed bikes that we see around the world today.

### RE-CYCLED FACT

#### Jan Gehl

The Danish architect Jan Gehl has done as much as anybody to improve the quality of urban life for cyclists and pedestrians alike, because he has always thought about urban planning from the point of view of the people who live in towns and cities (as opposed to most urban planners, who think about it from the point of view of traffic efficiency). He helped to transform the streets and public spaces of Copenhagen over a 40-year period and went on to design similar improvements in towns and cities around the world, including in Australia, New Zealand, the USA, South America, Russia, Jordan, Singapore and Britain (including one of Britain's first shared-space streets, New Road in Brighton).

Much of his focus has been on the bicycle, which he thinks will continue to play a growing part in people's lives owing to higher petrol prices, an increased awareness of the benefits of an active life and the fact that it's faster to get around urban environments by bike due to increasing traffic jams.

### Montreal, Canada

Montreal introduced the first self-service urban bike-sharing infrastructure in North America, with over 700 km (435 miles) of cycle paths and growing. Many of the downtown lanes are separated from cars by substantial concrete kerbs, and the city has become so bicycle-friendly that there have been complaints in winter from motorists about snow being cleared from cycle lanes first. The Montreal scheme, known as the BIXI programme, proved so successful that it has since been rolled out in London, Melbourne, Minneapolis and Washington. The city's greater metropolitan area also boasts a staggering 3,840 km (2,400 miles) of cycle trails, with plans to expand even further.

### Tokyo, Japan

Tokyo doesn't have as many dedicated cycle paths as some other cities, but its renowned urban-planning skills continue to create self-contained communities that require only short journeys to reach shops, schools and businesses, with many narrow shopping streets closed to traffic from their inception. Coupled with a very efficient rail network for longer distances, cycling is an integral part of the city's culture because most residents would have no need for a car even if they could afford one (which most of them can't).

Bike-sharing schemes and cycle paths for tourists are on the increase, having been given a boost as part of the infrastructure required to host the 2020 Tokyo Olympic Games.

### RE-CYCLED FACT

#### O sole mio!

The award for 'Most Brilliant Bike Scheme Initiative in the World Ever' must surely go to Trondheim, Norway, for the Trampe bicycle lift, the contraption that takes cyclists up one of its steepest hills. While still sitting on their bikes, riders place the sole of their right foot on one of the moving blocks in a 'tramline' at the edge of the pavement, whereupon the block propels the right foot and everything attached to it to the top of the 1:5 gradient at a speed of 6.4 km/h (4 mph).

### Paris, France

The Vélib scheme in Paris was one of the first mass-participation bike-rental systems anywhere in the world, and remains one of the biggest, with more than 20,000 bikes and around 1,800 stations covering the city. 'Vélib' is a portmanteau of the French for bike (*vélo*) and freedom (*liberté*). The operators face a constant battle to address the two main problems of the scheme: the number of bikes that are stolen (they seem to turn up a lot in Eastern Europe and North Africa); and the problem with bike distribution in the hillier parts of the city – nobody wants to cycle up to Montmartre, but everybody wants to cycle back down.

### Bogotá, Colombia

With less than 15 per cent of residents able to afford cars, bikes are something of a necessity to get around a city like Bogotá Colombia, whether it's safe or not. A culture of disrespect for traffic laws and the safety of cyclists still prevails among the city's drivers, resulting in the deaths of hundreds of cyclists each year, so the introduction of safe cycle lanes is as important here as it is anywhere. The city council has already provided over 480 km (300 miles) of cycle lanes, with plans for many more. When 110 km (70 miles) of the city's streets are closed to cars each Sunday over one million residents turn out to enjoy the weekly freedom of safe riding.

### RE-CYCLED FACT

#### Car-free equals carefree

Since 2011, La Paz and other cities across Bolivia have been closing their streets to traffic for a day each year, which temporarily drops the normal levels of air pollution by 70 per cent. Pedestrians and cyclists enjoy their most carefree day of the year, and strips of artificial turf are laid on top of the roads to encourage ball games. The car-free day goes by the magnificent title of 'Day of the Pedestrian and Cyclist in Defence of Mother Earth'.

### Groningen, the Netherlands

There is a definite trend in European cities in particular to increase the number of journeys that are made by bicycle, but not many cities can compete with the university city of Groningen in the very far north of the Netherlands. Since digging up a six-lane motorway intersection in the city centre in 1977 and replacing it with greenery, pedestrianisation, cycleways and bus lanes, it has achieved a journey-by-bike rate of more than

60 per cent. Much to the surprise of its many detractors at the time, this also resulted in an economic recovery for the city, as cyclists and bus users returned to city-centre shops and restaurants that they could previously get nowhere near in their cars.

## RE-CYCLED FACT

### Thriving bike cities

According to the Bicycle Friendly Cities Index in 2017, the top 20 cities around the world that are doing the most to improve their cycling infrastructure are as follows:

1. Copenhagen, Denmark
2. Utrecht, Netherlands
3. Amsterdam, Netherlands
4. Strasbourg, France
5. Malmö, Sweden
6. Bordeaux, France
7. Antwerp, Belgium
8. Ljubljana, Slovenia
9. Tokyo, Japan
10. Berlin, Germany
11. Barcelona, Spain
12. Vienna, Austria
13. Paris, France
14. Seville, Spain
15. Munich, Germany
16. Nantes, France
17. Hamburg, Germany
18. Helsinki, Finland
19. Oslo, Norway
20. Montreal, Canada

# CHAPTER 4

# *GREAT BIKE TRIPS IN BRITAIN AND BEYOND*

*It's by riding a bicycle you learn the contours of a country...
in a car only a high hill impresses...*

Ernest Hemingway, American author and journalist

There is no shortage of great bike trips in most of the world's countries. Some are not at all taxing and therefore ideal for beginners, families and fun riders; others are not for the faint-hearted, such as epic Alpine climbs and challenging Arctic forest tracks. In this chapter, we will look at a variety of interesting rides in Britain, mainland Europe and beyond.

## *OUT AND ABOUT IN THE BRITISH COUNTRYSIDE*

Away from British towns and cities, more and more cycle paths have been created along the sides of canals and rivers, through national parks, and on top of railway lines abandoned by the short-sighted politics of the 1960s, when the infamous Beeching report heralded the closure of half of the UK's railway stations and a third of its railway tracks in favour of increased road transport. Here is a short selection of some of the UK's most scenic bike rides.

### Tudor Trail, Kent

**Route**: Tonbridge Castle via Penshurst Place to Hever Castle

**Distance**: 10 miles (16 km)

**Time to allow**: 2 hours

**What to expect**: Pretty much traffic-free once you leave Tonbridge; a mixture of off-road (country park), woodland trail and country lanes.

**What you see**: Haysden Country Park, including Barden Lake; River Medway; Penshurst Place estate; villages of Penshurst, Chiddingstone and Hever; Hever Castle.

### Kennet and Avon Canal

**Route**: Bath to Reading

**Distance**: 85 miles (136 km)

**Time to allow**: 2–3 days

**What to expect**: Easy to moderate cycling along towpaths, country lanes and cycle paths.

**What you see**: Bath; canal locks (including a flight of sixteen at Caen Hill); houseboats; aqueducts at Dundas and Avoncliff; the market town of Devizes; North Wessex Downs; southern tip of the Cotswolds.

## Round the Island Cycle Route, Isle of Wight

**Route**: East Cowes to East Cowes (circular)

**Distance**: 62 miles (99 km)

**Time to allow**: 2–3 days (1 day if you're in a hurry and relatively fit)

**What to expect**: Mostly flat with moderate climbing on cycle paths, country lanes and through towns and villages.

**What you see**: Cowes; yachts; sea views; Freshwater Bay; the Needles; pretty villages; red squirrels.

## West Country Way

**Route**: Padstow Harbour to Bath or Bristol

**Distance**: 240 miles (384 km)

**Time to allow**: 7–9 days

**What to expect**: Mixture of roads, cycle paths, towpath and woodland; moderately to very hilly at times.

**What you see**: Camel Estuary; British Cycling Museum (near Camelford); Bodmin Moor; Exmoor; Somerset Levels; Glastonbury; Wells; Mendip Hills; Bath or Bristol; canals; sea views; birdlife.

## C2C (meaning Sea to Sea)

**Route**: Workington, Whitehaven or St Bees to Tynemouth or Sunderland

**Distance**: 140 miles (224 km)

**Time to allow**: 3–5 days (can be done in 1–2 days if you're hard enough)

**What to expect**: Tough cycling, especially across the Pennines – even tougher if you want to travel east to west into the prevailing wind. Surfaces include minor roads, disused railway lines and specially constructed off-road tracks.

**What you see**: Irish Sea (off Cumbrian coast); Lake District; Castlerigg stone circle; heather moors; Greystoke Castle (home of 'Tarzan'); rugged mountains; the highest cafe in England; North Sea (off Northumberland coast).

Note: The C2C is one of five sea-to-sea routes across the north of England, the narrowest part of mainland Britain. The second most popular after the C2C is the Way of the Roses, which runs from the statue of Eric Morecambe on the promenade of the town from which he took his stage name, over the very tough climbs of the Yorkshire Dales and on to Sunderland.

---

### Causeway Coast, Northern Ireland

**Route**: Ballycastle to Giant's Causeway and return to Ballycastle via Armoy

**Distance**: 35 miles (56 km)

**Time to allow**: A leisurely few hours to take in the sights.

**What to expect**: Coastal roads on the way to the Giant's Causeway, hill roads on the way back to Ballycastle.

**What you see**: Ballycastle; Kinbane Castle; Carrick-a-Rede rope bridge; Ballintoy Harbour; Whitepark Bay; Dunseverick Castle; Giant's Causeway; the Old Bushmills Distillery; Bushfoot Golf Club.

---

### Aviemore to Braemar, Scottish Highlands

**Route**: Aviemore to Braemar

**Distance**: 50 miles (80 km)

**Time to allow**: 1–2 days

**What to expect**: A road route through the Cairngorms National Park, which, as you might expect, is more than a wee bit hilly in places.

**What you see**: Aviemore village; the stunning scenery of the Scottish Highlands, including Ben Macdui, the second-highest mountain in the UK; heather moors; Glenlivet and Tomintoul whisky distilleries; Grantown-on-Spey village; Braemar village; Balmoral Castle.

## North Wales Coastal Route

**Route**: Holyhead to Chester

**Distance**: 108 miles (173 km)

**Time to allow**: 2–3 days

**What to expect**: Everything from roads to quiet lanes, towpaths, sea promenades and old railway lines. A 3-mile (5-km) section around Colwyn Bay is traffic-free. Mostly flat, but can get very windy, especially if you travel east to west into the prevailing wind.

**What you see**: Isle of Anglesey; Menai Strait; Snowdonia; seaside towns; beautiful coastline; sweeping views over Colwyn Bay; city of Chester.

## Windsor Circular via Windsor Great Park, Berkshire

**Route**: Windsor Castle to Windsor Castle (circular)

**Distance**: 15 miles (23 km)

**Time to allow**: 1 hour 30 minutes

**What to expect**: With mostly traffic-free minor roads, this is a great route for visitors and tourists wanting to see some iconic sights.

**What you see**: Windsor Castle; Windsor Great Park; Old Windsor; Eton College; River Thames; London skyline.

# GREAT BIKE TRIPS IN EUROPE

With such diverse topography and climates, Europe offers the cyclist everything from riverside meanders to epic mountain climbs and snow-covered forests. Here is a small selection to whet your appetite for some continental touring.

## On the other side of the Channel

**Route**: St Malo–Dinan–Rennes–Fougères–Mont-Saint-Michel–St Malo (circular)

**Distance**: 304 km (190 miles)

**Time to allow**: 4–6 days

**What to expect**: Relatively flat, some rolling countryside. Includes three separate long-distance traffic-free cycle paths, one following a river then a canal, one on disused railway lines, one on dykes across marshland.

**What you see**: Harbour town of St Malo; walled citadels; medieval châteaux; charming towns; coastal windmills; the World Heritage Site of Mont-Saint-Michel.

## Camino de Santiago

**Route**: French/Spanish border to Santiago de Compostela

**Distance**: 800 km (500 miles)

**Time to allow**: 1–2 weeks

**What to expect**: Mountain climbs and descents, plains and undulating countryside. You can choose from the off-road walkers' route (a mixture of shale, farm tracks and baked earth or mud, depending on the season) or the parallel-running road route, or a mixture of the two. It's not all that hilly except for three big climbs, including the initial one over the Pyrenees (you're on a pilgrimage route, so it's only fair you should suffer a bit).

**What you see**: The stunning scenery of the Pyrenees; Roncesvalles monastery; Pamplona; Roman roads and bridges; free wine fountain at Bodegas Irache; ancient rural villages, including the mountaintop village of O Cebreiro with its ancient thatched huts; Santiago de Compostela Cathedral.

## The challenge of the Stelvio

**Route**: Innsbruck, Austria to Monaco

**Distance**: 800 km (500 miles)

**Time to allow**: 7 days

**What to expect**: 11,300 metres (37,000 feet) of climbing, including the Passo dello Stelvio, the second-highest paved road in Europe (and, perhaps needless to say, the same amount of fast descending).

**What you see**: The Eastern Alps; Innsbruck; St Moritz; Lugano; Lake Como; Italian Riviera; French Riviera; Principality of Monaco.

### RE-CYCLED FACT

### Passo dello Stelvio (Stelvio Pass)

The Passo dello Stelvio is famous for its 75 hairpin bends, 48 on one side and 27 on the other. It has been crossed 12 times by the Giro d'Italia, for the first time in 1953, when the legendary Italian rider Fausto Coppi won the stage, and it is the highest point reached by any of the three Grand Tours (Giro d'Italia, Tour de France and Vuelta a España). Each year the pass is closed to motor traffic for one day in late August, when around 8,000 cyclists take the opportunity to ride to the top.

## Beer and bikes in Austria and Germany

**Route**: Salzburg to Passau

**Distance**: 235 km (146 miles)

**Time to allow**: 6 days

**What to expect**: Moderate cycling along undulating river valleys, leisurely beer-tasting at any number of breweries and a beer bath in the Landhotel Moorhof in Franking (this isn't a bath full of beer; it's a bath containing beer extract, which detoxifies the body and relieves problems with circulation in the hands and feet, which is quite useful if you're on a cycling trip). From Passau, there's the added bonus of the Danube cycle path to the famous Trappist brewery at Engelhartszell.

**What you see**: Austrian Lake District; Bavaria; bottle-green rivers; nature reserve; a Benedictine abbey; pretty town squares; breweries and more breweries.

## Winter fatbiking in Finland

**Route**: Various, including trails in Oulanka and Pyhä-Luosto national parks

**Distance**: Various

**Time to allow**: Rent fatbikes by the hour or go on a guided tour for a week.

**What to expect**: Huge levels of fun cycling on snow through pine forests and on frozen lakes.

**What you see**: Christmas-card scenery complete with log cabins; reindeer in the wild and on your plate; bemused Russian border guards on snowmobiles; imprints in the snow that are the exact shape of a bicycle and its rider; the Northern Lights (if you're lucky).

## RE-CYCLED FACT

### Fatbikes

Fatbikes are mountain bikes with really fat, deep-tread tyres to allow grip on loose or slippery surfaces, including snow, ice and sand. As soon as you gain the confidence to release your death-grip on the handlebar, your loose steering of the bike and the low pressure of your tyres will enable you to perform manoeuvres that you could only dream of on terra firma. If you do fall off, your landing will be a soft one as long as you manage to avoid obstacles such as pine trees if you're in a snow-covered forest. If you fall off on a frozen lake, your landing will be a bit harder, but you'll be wearing clothing more akin to skiwear than Lycra, so even then your pride is the only thing that won't be cushioned to some extent.

The capabilities of fatbikes (variations include touring versions, tricycles and e-fatbikes) are such that they have been used to cross Alaska in winter and have even turned up at the South Pole. They are used for commuting in all seasons in the northernmost parts of the world, including Canada, Finland, Norway, Sweden and Alaska. In the contiguous USA, any excuse will do to get the fatbike out, from riding the riverbanks of the Mississippi to the sand dunes of New Mexico.

## GREAT BIKE TRIPS IN THE REST OF THE WORLD

For cyclists who like to go even further afield, the choice is almost bewildering, from iconic American road trips to the paddy fields of South East Asia or a two-wheel safari in East Africa. Here are just five to add to your bucket list.

### Bicycle Route 66

**Route**: Flagstaff, Arizona to Las Vegas, Nevada

**Distance**: 263 miles (420 km)

**Time to allow**: 8 days

**What to expect**: Challenging climbs, wonderfully long descents and a finishing line of your choice on the Las Vegas Strip – perhaps alongside the half-size Eiffel Tower to end your trip on a Tour de France note. Much of the route is traffic-free and virtually none of it involves heavy traffic (although you might see a few cars on the Strip).

**What you see**: The Grand Canyon and Colorado River; Hoover Dam and Lake Mead; the spectacular desert and rocky gorges of Arizona and Nevada (think cowboy films); tumbleweed; historic pioneer towns; 1960s filling stations; a Native American trading post; prairie dogs; birds of prey; more tumbleweed.

Note: If you have the time and energy to go the whole hog and ride Bicycle Route 66 in its entirety from Chicago, Illinois to Santa Monica Pier in California, you will pedal across eight states for 2,448 miles (3,940 km). My tip would be to cycle it from west to east, i.e. from Santa Monica to Chicago, because that is also the direction of the prevailing wind. Bicycle Route 66 sticks as close as possible to the original four-wheeled version, but diverges where necessary to remain bike-friendly.

## Saddle safari in Tanzania

**Route**: Arusha (West Kilimanjaro) to Pangani Town on the Indian Ocean
**Distance**: 470 km (290 miles)

**Time to allow**: 11 days (cycling tours of shorter duration are also available, starting at 4 days)

**What to expect**: Riding through magnificent savannah, tropical forest and lush highlands, and nights in campsites or lodges (depending on your tour). It will be reasonably hot by day and cool by night, so you need to have layers. Many tours take a day or two off from cycling to allow 4×4 tours into the safari parks that are off limits to bike riders (to save them from getting all eaten up by lions).

**What you see**: Coffee and banana plantations; palm fields; acacia trees; colourful Maasai villages and markets; the Serengeti grasslands; Mount Kilimanjaro; the Great Rift Valley; more wildlife and birdlife than you ever thought possible to see sitting on a saddle; the Indian Ocean.

## The Dubai desert

**Route**: Al Qudra Bike Track ('the Lollipop')

**Distance**: 86 km (53 miles)

**Time to allow**: 3–4 hours to cycle the entire lollipop (up the stick, round the lollipop and back down the stick to the start), although there is parking that allows you to ride just the lollipop without the stick.

**What to expect**: An extraordinary place to cycle, with glass-smooth tarmac cutting through the desert – it's ideal for leisurely cycling or for honing your time-trialling skills. The midday sunshine and heat are best avoided and getting up before dawn will in any event reward you with a glorious sunrise.

Evenings are also good but only the stick is lit. There is a Trek bike shop and a cafe at the start that totally buzz on weekend mornings, and there are gazebo rest stops around the track if you need some shade.

There aren't many hills, but that means wind, which becomes stronger as the day progresses (another reason to avoid the middle of the day, as dust storms reduce visibility and penetrate your clothes and orifices). If you do get into trouble, there is good reception for your mobile phone and a rescue quad bike on standby to come and pick you up.

**What you see**: Sand; ghaf (evergreen, drought-resistant trees that dot the route); Sheikh Mohammed's ranch (and possibly even 'Sheikh Mo' himself, as he sometimes uses the track); the Dubai skyline; Al Qudra Lakes; the enormous radar dishes of the James Bond-style solar power station that keeps Dubai air-conditioned by day and lit by night; camels; herds of Arabian oryx; more sand.

## Dubai's cycling infrastructure

You may think it well-nigh impossible to build a cycling infrastructure in and around a city of huge hotels and shopping malls surrounded by desert on three sides and the Persian Gulf on the other, but many people probably thought the same thing about building a ski slope in Dubai.

It's true that there are only limited opportunities for cycling around the city's streets, but the track at Al Qudra has now been linked by a 21-km (13-mile) path, known as The Stick, to the 8-km (5-mile) former camel-racing track in the middle of the city, which is now the District One Cycling and Running Track. Cycle paths and bike-rental stations are being added all the time, in particular to provide links to the city's parks and malls.

It's not just tourists who are drawn to this unique cycling infrastructure, because many locals have been inspired to take up the sport since the first running of the annual Dubai Tour in 2014. They've watched some of the world's top cyclists race along their palm-tree-lined avenues and they've witnessed at first hand the sprint finishes of Mark Cavendish and Marcel Kittel in the shadow of the Burj Khalifa.

Cycling organisations have sprouted up, including the female-only Velo Vixens club, and top-of-the-range bikes are becoming the newest status symbol – if you drive a high-end car, you want to put a high-end bike on it, and it's not unusual to see a Ferrari or Lamborghini with a bike rack on it.

## Vietnam to Laos on a bike

**Route**: Hanoi to Luang Prabang

**Distance**: 507 km (315 miles)

**Time to allow**: 8 days

**What to expect**: A reasonable level of fitness is required to cycle in the heat and humidity of South East Asia. The available trails range from flat with some downhill to very hilly indeed if you want to include some of the mountain trails.

**What you see**: City of Hanoi and the Red River; unspoiled local villages; saffron-clad monks; Indochinese villas; paddy fields; green mountains; the Mekong River and the gilded temples of Luang Prabang's World Heritage Site.

## Ride like the (Tasmanian) devil

**Route**: Top of Mount Wellington to Hobart

**Distance**: 21 km (13 miles)

**Time to allow**: Up to 2 hours 30 minutes for each descent

**What to expect**: Spectacular views and huge fun descending from an elevation of 1,270 metres (4,160 feet) at whatever speed you're comfortable with, which may depend on the strength of your wrists as much as anything. It will be Alpine cold on top of the mountain and become warmer as you descend through verdant forest, so you'll need at least one extra layer at the start of the ride. There is an optional 5-km (3-mile) off-road dirt-trail section in the foothills on the way down for the more adventurous.

If you want to get some fitness training in as well, feel free to cycle up the average 6 per cent (maximum 9 per cent) gradient before or after the descent. You will be following in the pedals of Cadel Evans and Richie Porte, both of whom have won a mountaintop stage here. The climb is fairly gruelling, not least because the surface is a bit rough.

**What you see**: Panoramic vista of Hobart, the Tasman Peninsula and the River Derwent; weird rock formations; birds of prey; gum trees; Hobart suburbs and waterfront.

## Bikepacking

Bikepacking is a new trend that combines mountain biking with touring, so if long-distance, off-road trails sound like they might be your thing, you have the potential to become a bikepacker.

What makes bikepacking possible is the lighter gear that's now available for the purpose, i.e. gear that can be carried without the need to mount heavy racks and panniers, which can cause problems with balance, steering and suspension on off-road trails (they also make your bike too heavy to lug up and down terrain that cannot be cycled). The new, lighter gear includes lightweight roll-bags that can be carried on the handlebar and/or on the top of a rear rack, useful for carrying your lightweight tent and lightweight sleeping bag (can you see a theme developing here?); lightweight frame bags, especially useful for on-the-go snacks; expandable, slimline seat bags; and a lightweight backpack for bulkier but lighter items or weight that will reduce as the day progresses (i.e. food and water).

The only other essential requirement to becoming a bikepacker is a mindset that allows you to pack in minimalist fashion. In other words, you need to be able to make do with the bare necessities of life, which is the main reason I won't be suggesting bikepacking to my wife anytime soon.

Note: The selected bike trips in this chapter are clearly not intended as detailed route planners, so be sure to check relevant maps, guides and websites before setting off. By way of example, the Sustrans charity (www.sustrans.org.uk) runs and provides details of the entire National Cycling Network around Britain and has partnered itself with the EuroVelo project (www.eurovelo.com) to establish international cycling routes across Europe. For information on the growing network of routes around and across the USA, check out the Adventure Cycling Association (www.adventurecycling.org).

# CHAPTER 5

# *IN THE CLUB*

---

*The friendship and camaraderie you have with other
cyclists is the be-all and end-all of your life.*

Tommy Godwin, double bronze-medal winner at the 1948 London Olympics

## *CYCLING CLUBS*

Cycling clubs sprang up in the nineteenth century as quickly as manufacturers could make bikes. Many of those who joined the clubs would have experienced for the first time the joy that comes from a shared hobby, a camaraderie that was often less class-ridden than that of other clubs of the day, and a feeling of safety in numbers (it was not uncommon for early bike riders to have insults or even stones thrown at them by those who couldn't or didn't want to join in the fun).

Cycling clubs really took off in a big way with the arrival of penny-farthings in the 1870s, and it must have been a sight to behold when hundreds of them rolled along together into the countryside at weekends.

Women were not excluded from the early cycling clubs, although they did sometimes find themselves barred from the social side of things. It was 1922 before the first women-only club was established in the UK (the Rosslyn Ladies Cycling Club in Essex) and 1956 before the Women's Cycle Racing Association was formed.

Many clubs were set up for the benefit of specific sectors of society, like civil servants, ex-servicemen, card-holding communists or adherents of a particular religion. Many had self-evident names, like the Brent Jewish Road Club, the Vegetarian Cycling and Athletic Club, the Theatrical United Cycling Club and the more recently formed No. 1 Muslim Ladies' Cycling Club in East London, which was set up in 2005.

Nowadays, of course, there are clubs for more than just road cycling. There are those that cater specifically for (a combination of) road, track or off-road pursuits, or for the increasingly popular sport of triathlon, which includes cycling along with running and swimming. Perhaps you fancy having a go at cycle speedway, the format of which is pretty much the same as the motorised version, or cyclo-cross, a gruelling cross-country affair which involves having to dismount to carry your bike over obstacles before setting off again on two wheels.

## AWAY FROM THE MAINSTREAM

If your needs are rather more exotic than the mainstream cycling disciplines, consider the following options:

### Bicycle polo

Bicycle polo clubs and leagues are springing up around the world. It was traditionally played on grass and looked like it was taking off when it was chosen as a sport for the London 1908 Olympics, but it never really did – until now. The modern hard-court version (indoor and outdoor) has caused a real spike in interest in countries as far apart as Britain, Malaysia, the USA, Australia, Nepal, Brazil and Cuba.

## Tandem riding

Tandem clubs exist for like-minded duos, from those who want to ride for fun in the country to those who want to do some serious touring. Membership will offer opportunities to attend events and rallies, and provide valuable advice on the practicalities of tandeming. Find out what it takes to be the captain on board, or whether you are more suited to the position of rear admiral (yes, it even has its own terminology).

## Tricycling

Don't be fooled – we're talking about a full programme of events for grown-ups here, at home and abroad, including regular competitions. The first point of contact in the UK is the Tricycle Association, formed in 1928 and still catering today for riders of modern and classic tricycles, and the clubs they belong to.

## Veteran bicycles

The Veteran-Cycle Club was formed in 1955 and today has worldwide membership of over 2,500, with many special-interest groups formed according to the types of cycles and/or marques that members are particularly enthusiastic about. Keeping the past alive for fans of everything from dandy-chargers and penny-farthings to folding bikes and Choppers, local, national and international events are a sight to behold.

### The Folding Society

Fancy rolling your Brompton M Type down to the Milton Keynes Origami and chilling out with fellow origamists who may have sneaked in on an Airnimal Chameleon or flown in on a Birdy? If you have answered 'yes', you need to join the Folding Society, which is for all those with an interest in folding bicycles. You can of course travel to any of the Origami Rides by car or train and simply unfold when you get there.

### The British Human Power Club

This club organises events and competitions for leg-powered or arm-powered two-, three- and four-wheeled cycles. Go the whole hog and build yourself a full fairing (any structure added to a vehicle to improve streamlining is a 'fairing'). Recumbent bikes are especially popular in the human-power world, because low-profile plus fairing equals speed!

### Bombay Bicycle Club

OK, they're actually an indie rock band from London, but they're better than good so check them out for your on-bike playlist!

## TWO WHEELS, TOO EASY?

If even two wheels seem like one too many to you, perhaps you should think about taking up a unicycling activity or sport. Touring unicycles are available if you want to go round the world on one. If you dream of joining the circus or performing at London's Covent Garden, you might want to try out a giraffe (with the saddle up to 10 feet/3 metres high); a kangaroo (both feet move in the same parallel direction); or a freestyle (with or without juggling clubs).

But if you would prefer to join a club and take part in an individual or team sport, there are a number of options there as well. The International Unicycling Federation sets the rules for a number of one-wheeled sports, including:

### Track events

These range from 100 metres to marathon distance, plus slalom, high jump and long jump. But if you find these a bit easy-peasy, try one of these speciality events:

- The 30-metre walk-the-wheel (you have to push the tyre with your feet as opposed to using the pedals).

- The 50-metre one-foot (you're allowed to use both pedals for the first 5 metres, but then your foot of choice is on its own all the way to the finish line).

- The slow backward (what it says).

### Mountain unicycling (MUni)

Mountain unicycling is an adventure sport that includes cross-country, uphill and downhill. You won't be surprised to learn that you need a strong core and better-than-average balance to be good at any of these disciplines!

---

### One-wheeled wonder

The Canadian godfather of off-road unicycling, Kris Holm, was the founder and former world champion of unicycle trials (obstacle riding), and he has unicycled to the summits of volcanoes and mountains around the world. Strong leg muscles, do you think?

---

## Artistic unicycling

Artistic unicycling consists of freestyle events (not dissimilar in format to ice figure skating) for individuals, pairs, groups of three to eight and groups of over eight contestants (a group of twenty is not uncommon). Unicyclists execute their routines, including synchronised moves in the case of groups, to preselected music.

## Unicycle hockey

Using ice hockey sticks and a ball, unicycle hockey is played as far afield as Australia, Korea and Sweden, and there are competitive leagues in the UK, Germany and Switzerland.

### Unicycle basketball

This is exactly what you would expect it to be and probably every bit as much fun as it looks. The sport is unsurprisingly popular in the USA and Canada, but the Puerto Rico All Stars have been one of the most dominant teams in the world.

---

If you live in the UK, check out the Union of UK Unicyclists website (www.unicycle.org.uk) for information about clubs in your area, and, just in case you're thinking that unicycling is just for the geeks of the cycling world, check out Chapter 10 (Famous Easy Riders) for a surprising list of famous unicyclists.

---

## EVENTS AND FESTIVALS

One of the many advantages of belonging to a cycling club is that it opens up access to special (mostly road) events – but you don't have to belong to a club to participate in many of these, or in the growing number of cycling festivals that are springing up. Here is a selection to whet your appetite:

### One-day 'classics'

*London–Brighton*

This annual 54-mile (86-km) charity race on behalf of the British Heart Foundation attracts around 30,000 riders. It starts in Clapham Common and rolls through the pleasant, but hilly, countryside of Surrey and Sussex, with its sting in the tail coming with the need to climb the South Downs at Ditchling Beacon before the descent to Brighton seafront. There is also a 75-mile (120-km) off-road version for mountain-bike riders.

## Tweed Run

This annual group bike ride through London has been copied in dozens of cities in every paved continent of the world, including Glasgow, Manchester and Birmingham in the UK. Some of the unexpected cities to have taken part around the globe are St Petersburg (Russia), Spetses (Greece), Fremantle (Australia), Chihuahua (Mexico) and Tokyo (Japan). Cyclists invoke memories of a bygone age by dressing in period tweed costume (preferably 'plus fours' for the men) and ride vintage or modern bicycles through the streets of their respective cities.

## World Naked Bike Ride

This is now held annually in over 50 cities in 20 countries worldwide. Brighton, York, Cardiff, Edinburgh, Newcastle and London were among the UK's 18 participating cities in 2017. Other cities have included Melbourne, Cape Town, San Francisco and Portland, Oregon, which regularly claims to have the most participants (up to 10,000). The general idea is to remind the world that it has become too oil- and car-dependent, and to stress to the world's motorists in particular that cyclists are made of vulnerable flesh and bone. If you don't want to go the whole hog, body paint and/or underpants can be used to disguise your really naughty bits.

## Dunwich Dynamo

This overnight (and hopefully moonlit) ride of 120 miles (192 km) stretches from Hackney in East London to Dunwich on the Suffolk coast. Its popularity has led to similar through-the-night rides elsewhere, including the Exmouth Exodus from Bath to the Devon coast and the London Ride the Night event (see following entry).

## Women who're making a real difference

Breeze Bike Rides is a British Cycling initiative to get more women riding and taking part in mass-participation events such as Sky Ride City and Sky Ride Local, and in women-only events like the Cycletta, a series of challenging but achievable sportives (this just means 'non-competitive') in aid of Macmillan Cancer Support. Another growing event is the Women v. Cancer Ride the Night event after dark through the streets of London. The same charity is now also organising a London to Paris event and even some rides much further afield, like its 2018 event in India, starting at the Taj Mahal and finishing in the appropriately named Pink City of Jaipur, where their signature pink cycling attire or accessories should blend in very nicely indeed.

## Pedal for Scotland

This 110-mile (176-km) challenge sees riders make their way from Glasgow to the Scottish capital, Edinburgh. A sportive takes place at the same time, but on a parallel route to allow the challenge riders a clear run.

## Wiggle Dragon Ride L'Etape Wales

This prestigious annual Welsh sportive leaves from Margam Country Park, Port Talbot. There are four routes to accommodate riders of all abilities, with the Brecon Beacons supplying the toughest climbs for those who like a bit of a challenge:

- Dragon Devil: 186 miles (300 km)
- Gran Fondo: 140 miles (225 km)
- Medio Fondo: 95 miles (153 km)
- Macmillan 100: 62 miles (100 km)

## RideLondon

This showcase three-day cycling festival run for charity is the equivalent of the London Marathon for cyclists, with Olympic-style road racing thrown in. The format, which continues to evolve from one year to the next, runs something like this:

- The London–Surrey Classic, a 125-mile (200-km) one-day race around London and Surrey, featuring many of the world's top male professional riders, including Olympians and well-known Tour de France riders.

- The RideLondon Classique, involving laps around a central London circuit that takes in many of the city's iconic sites. It has the largest prize fund of any one-day race in the women's professional cycling calendar.

- The RideLondon Surrey 100, a 100-mile (160-km) traffic-free sportive primarily over the Classic route.

- The RideLondon Surrey 46, a shorter version of the 100, run as a sportive over 46 miles (74 km) for less-competitive riders and the 16–18 age group not yet eligible to enter the Surrey 100.

- The FreeCycle, a 5-mile (8-km) fun ride around the closed streets of the capital, with festival zones dotted around the route. Music and other forms of entertainment abound, including BMX stunt shows, penny-farthing trials and a bike try-out area.

- The Grand Prix, a series of junior and disabled (handcycling) races at the Lee Valley VeloPark in Queen Elizabeth Olympic Park, which also has a festival zone.

- The RideLondon Cycle Show at the London ExCel exhibition centre.

*L'Etape du Tour*
This annual charity-based event runs over one of the Tour de France stages for the year in question. It will take you a lot longer than the actual Tour riders to complete the stage, but the sense of achievement is still going to be huge.

There is a host of other one-day road races and sportives throughout the year for the more serious club cyclist, including magnificently named ones like the Dartmoor Demon, Exmouth Exterminator, Wye Valley

Warrior, South Downs Epic, Fell Beast, Lakeland Monster Miles and Devil's Rampage MTB. End-of-season sportives include the appropriately named Fallen Leaves, which encompasses road, mountain-bike and cyclo-cross events. Or why not join the organised day trips over the Channel to try the French Revolution? With some of these events, you can just turn up on the day and go. Others (like the French trip) will sell out their several hundred places within days. Check the www.ukcyclingevents.co.uk and www.britishcycling.org.uk websites for more information.

## Longer events

### John O'Groats to Land's End (JOGLE)

Also known as the 'End to End' or 'Deloitte Ride Across Britain', over 700 riders take part each year and more than 90 per cent of them make it to the finish line after 969 miles (1,560 km) of cycling. If you're pushed for time, energy or willpower, you can confine yourself to the four-day Scottish or five-day English package. Or feel free to reverse the whole route and do the LEJOG as opposed to the JOGLE – just don't forget that it's uphill to Scotland and that you'll be saving the Highlands for near the end of the ride.

### London to Paris

Join more than a hundred like-minded cyclists to ride just over 300 miles (500 km) from a chosen London location to the Eiffel Tower and raise money for the charity of your choice. After four days of riding to the French capital, the return journey is by Eurostar.

*Bike Week*

Bike Week sees a series of cycle-themed events take place around the UK for one week in the summer. Events range from fun rides on streets closed to traffic, skills training, guided rides, commuter and workplace-based challenges, cycle fairs, themed rides, indoor track trials and even cycle speed dating. Check out www.bikeweek.org.uk for events near you.

*Package holiday*

Or if you want cycling to be an integral part of your well-earned holiday, search the web for the many tailored cycling tours that are available as a holiday package, at home or abroad. See the previous Great Bike Trips chapter for inspiration.

# CHAPTER 6

# *BIKE RACING*

*When my legs hurt, I say 'Shut up, legs!
Do what I tell you to do!'*

Jens Voigt, former German professional road racer
(and candidate for most popular German on the planet)

Road and track racing took off in a big way in continental Europe in the late nineteenth century, while Victorian Britain was still being positively Victorian about the whole thing. Without the backing of the establishment, bike racing didn't take off in Britain until much later. Speed was seen as a continental thing, best left to those volatile Europeans and their modern ways.

The world's first organised road race ran from Paris to Rouen in 1869, when the rules stated that riders were not allowed to use sails or be pulled by a dog. The race was won by an Englishman, James Moore, not least because he alone had the advantage of ball bearings in his moving parts (or, at least, in the moving parts of his bike). But even he had to get off and push his bike up the steeper climbs, gears not yet having been invented.

Some of the 'classic' one-day road races that are still going strong today followed soon after, including Liège–Bastogne–Liège (1894) and Paris–Roubaix (1896).

Stage racing over several days or weeks took off with the inaugural Tour de France in 1903. Road races often finished with laps of a velodrome track, thereby combining the French love of both road and track racing.

The French and the Belgians were to dominate continental bike racing initially, but they were soon joined by the Italians and later the Spaniards. A 'Foreign Legion' of English-speaking cyclists would gradually arrive on the European road scene in the later part of the twentieth century, not least the Americans and, most recently, the Brits, whose Olympic success has now spilt over into professional road racing.

The Olympics, as you might expect, has always been a rather more cosmopolitan affair than the European racing scene, with the early medal winners of the twentieth century including Greek, South African, Swedish, American and British riders.

But bike racing was to go really global in the twenty-first century. Starting in January 2008, the Tour Down Under in and around Adelaide became the inaugural event of the UCI (Union Cycliste Internationale) calendar; the unprecedented road and track success of Great Britain at the Beijing, London and Rio Olympic Games looks like taking cycling to a whole new level; and BMX track racing became the newest Olympic sport of the time at the London Games in 2012, gripping millions around the world.

We will look at all of that, and more, in this chapter, but let us start where it all began – on the road.

# PART 1: ROAD

In this section we will look at some of the classic one-day road races as well as the longer stage races (also known as 'tours'). We will also cover road racing at the Olympic Games and World Championships.

## The classics

The classics are seriously tough one-day races that take place in western Europe in the spring and autumn, either side of the main stage-race season. If you're strong enough and hard enough to sweat blood and risk broken bones, immortal glory awaits. The five most prestigious classics are known as the 'Monuments', of which two are in Italy, two are in Belgium and one is in France.

### Milan–San Remo

First raced in 1907, this is the first true classic of the season, known in Italian as *La classica di primavera* ('the spring classic'). It is also known as the 'sprinters' classic' because it often ends in a mass sprint. The great Belgian Eddy Merckx holds the record for most wins (seven). The German Erik Zabel would have won his fifth Milan–San Remo in 2004 had he not lifted his arms too early to celebrate his 'victory', thereby allowing himself to be pipped at the post.

### Tour of Flanders

First run in 1913, the *Vlaanderens Mooiste* ('Flanders' finest') is one of the Monuments' two 'cobbled classics' (the other being the Paris–Roubaix), so called because of the stretches of cobbled roads that the riders have to contend with. Along with the Paris–Roubaix and the Liège–Bastogne–Liège, the Tour of Flanders is also one of the three so-called 'Ardennes classics'. It is said to be one of the most difficult races to ride, and therefore one of the most satisfying to win.

A women's race has been run on the same day as the men's since 2004. Britain's Nicole Cooke won it in 2007 and fellow Brit Lizzie Armitstead (now Deignan) won it in 2016. The 2013 race was won by Marianne Vos, the Dutchwoman who is generally regarded to be the best female bike rider of her generation.

### Paris–Roubaix

First held in 1896, and nicknamed *L'enfer du nord* ('Hell of the north'). Many riders will avoid it like the plague, because they don't want to risk early-season broken bones. For others, it is the ultimate prize. There are almost 30 bone-jarring cobbled sectors, including the Trouée d'Arenberg, a forested stretch of cobbles that dates back to the time of Napoleon I, and which is only opened twice a year – once to check that it is still far too dangerous to race on, and the other time for the race itself.

Two Belgians hold the record for most wins (four): Roger de Vlaeminck and Tom Boonen.

### Liège–Bastogne–Liège

The oldest classic of all, having been first run as a professional race in 1894. Known as *La Doyenne* ('Grand old dame'), this Belgian offering is arguably the toughest of the classics on account of its many hard climbs, particularly in the second half of the race. The route goes through the part of the Ardennes in which German and Allied forces fought out the Battle of the Bulge towards the end of World War Two. Most wins by a single rider is five, another record held by Eddy Merckx.

## Giro di Lombardia

First took place in 1905, and known as *La Classica delle foglie morte* ('Classic of the falling leaves') because it is held in northern Italy in the autumn. Although the signature symbol of the race has become Lake Como, it is known as the 'climbers' classic' because of the use it makes of the nearby mountains, and it has in fact been won most times (five) by the great Italian climber of the 1940s and 1950s, Fausto Coppi.

The rider who has won the most Monuments by far (19) is Eddy Merckx. Only three riders, all Belgian, have won all five during the course of their careers: Roger de Vlaeminck, Rik van Looy and, of course, Eddy Merckx himself. Britain's Tom Simpson won three different Monuments between 1961 and 1965 (Tour of Flanders, Milan–San Remo and Giro di Lombardia), with Mark Cavendish the only other British winner when he won the Milan–San Remo in 2009.

## RE-CYCLED FACT

### Il ne Passerieu pas

In 1907, the Frenchman Georges Passerieu still managed to win the Paris–Roubaix despite being stopped on his way into the stadium by a gendarme who wanted to check he had the correct tax plate on his bike. Passerieu's language at the time was later reported to have been 'colourful'.

## The Tours

Bicycle stage-racing doesn't come bigger than the three Grand Tours on the UCI (Union Cycliste Internationale) calendar:

- Tour de France

- Giro d'Italia

- Vuelta a España

Only supreme athletes have the strength, stamina and sheer willpower to survive stage after stage, day after day, of fast racing, often combined with tough mountain climbing. Only the very best of those survivors have what it takes to win.

The Tours each last for three weeks: the Giro in May/June; the Tour in June/July; and the Vuelta in September. And they each have three main prizes: the general classification (GC) for the all-rounders; the points classification for the sprinters; and the 'King of the Mountains' classification for the specialist climbers. To give you an idea of the scale of these races, consider the following statistical averages for each three-week event:

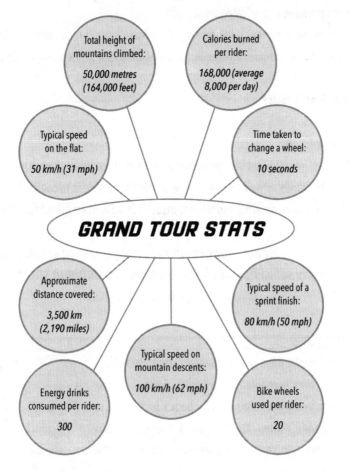

Total height of mountains climbed:

*50,000 metres (164,000 feet)*

Calories burned per rider:

*168,000 (average 8,000 per day)*

Typical speed on the flat:

*50 km/h (31 mph)*

Time taken to change a wheel:

*10 seconds*

**GRAND TOUR STATS**

Approximate distance covered:

*3,500 km (2,190 miles)*

Typical speed of a sprint finish:

*80 km/h (50 mph)*

Typical speed on mountain descents:

*100 km/h (62 mph)*

Energy drinks consumed per rider:

*300*

Bike wheels used per rider:

*20*

Other 'elite' (but much shorter) stage races include the Tour Down Under, Paris–Nice and the Critérium du Dauphiné. The next tour category (classified as 'majors') includes races as far apart as the Tour of California, the Tour de Langkawi (Malaysia) and the Tour of Turkey. The Tour of Britain was upgraded to this category in 2014.

The most important stage race on the women's circuit is currently the Giro d'Italia Internazionale Femminile, the only Grand Tour on the women's circuit.

## The Grand Tours

*Tour de France*
First run in 1903 and still the biggest and best bike race in the world, the Tour de France remains to cycling what the World Cup is to football, what Wimbledon is to tennis and what the Super Bowl is to American football.

> ***The Tour de France produces in me such persistent satisfaction that my saliva flows in imperceptible but stubborn streams.***
>
> Salvador Dalí, Catalan surrealist painter

<u>*Yellow jersey*</u>
The symbolic prize of the general classification (GC) is the coveted *maillot jaune* (yellow jersey), yellow having been the colour of the pages of the *L'Auto* newspaper owned by the Tour's founder, Henri Desgrange. Today the race always finishes on the

Champs-Élysées in Paris after around 3,500 km (2,190 miles) of time trials, flat stages and mountain climbs.

Four riders have won the yellow jersey competition five times:

- Jacques Anquetil (France)
- Bernard Hinault (France)
- Eddy Merckx (Belgium)
- Miguel Induráin (Spain)

Brian Robinson was the first Briton to finish a Tour de France, in 1955, and the first to win a stage, in 1958. Bradley Wiggins became the first British winner of the Tour in 2012, the latest in a long line of specialist time triallists who managed to hang on in the mountains to the advantages they gained against the clock back at sea level, and fellow British rider Chris Froome has entered the history books by winning the Tour four times in five years at the time of writing (see Hall of Fame later for more detail on Wiggins and Froome).

### RE-CYCLED FACT

#### From hero to zero

The American Lance Armstrong rewrote the record books when he won seven consecutive Tours between 1999 and 2005, albeit under a constant cloud of suspicion. In 2012, it was proven once and for all that he had taken drugs and engaged in blood-doping throughout his career, whereupon the authorities stripped him of his titles and Armstrong finally confessed all in an interview with Oprah Winfrey.

The story was told in the 2015 film *The Program*, with Armstrong played by Ben Foster, who took performance-enhancing drugs during shooting to better understand his role. The film was based on the 2012 book *Seven Deadly Sins: My Pursuit of Lance Armstrong*, written by *The Sunday Times* journalist David Walsh, who was played in the film by Chris O'Dowd.

### Green jersey (points classification for sprinters)

The German Erik Zabel remains the rider who has won the most green-jersey competitions, with a record six (consecutive) wins between 1996 and 2001, although at the time of writing in 2017 current Slovakian rider Peter Sagan is up to five wins.

British rider Mark Cavendish, aka the 'Manx Missile', is smashing the Tour individual sprint records as he chalks up stage win after stage win with his lightning bursts of speed to the finish line (see Hall of Fame later for more detail); he became the first British winner of the green-jersey competition in 2011.

## *Polka-dot jersey (King of the Mountains classification)*

Legendary Tour climbers include Lucien van Impe (Belgium) and Federico Bahamontes (Spain), who each won six King of the Mountains titles. The Frenchman Richard Virenque won seven, but his reputation was tarnished as a central figure in the infamous Festina doping affair in 1998. Scottish rider  Robert Millar won the King of the Mountains title in 1984, becoming the first rider from an English-speaking country to do so. Chris Froome became the second British winner in 2015 when he won the King of the Mountains competition along with the general classification.

Note: Robert Millar withdrew from public life after retirement from the sport in 1995 and re-emerged as part of the ITV4 Tour de France commentary team in 2017, but as Philippa York, having transitioned to life as a woman in the intervening years.

---

### La Course by Le Tour de France

After the demise of the women's version of the Tour de France stage race in 2009, La Course was initiated as a one-day race over 13 laps of the Champs-Élysées in 2014 ahead of the men's final Tour de France stage. It was won by Dutch superstar Marianne Vos.

In 2017, the event was stretched over two days to coincide with the eighteenth and twentieth stages of the men's race. The first day was a mountain stage, with the riders with the best times going forward to a pursuit stage in Marseille two days later. Britain's Lizzie Deignan finished second on both stages to Dutchwoman Annemiek van Vleuten.

Under its previous incarnation as a Grand Tour, the race was won twice by British rider Nicole Cooke (2006 and 2007) and once by fellow Brit Emma Pooley (2009).

### RE-CYCLED FACT

### Vive la Grande Bretagne!

In 2007, when the Tour de France visited Britain for the third time, millions lined the streets of London and the roads to Canterbury, an indication that road racing had finally entered the British consciousness at something like the levels enjoyed in mainland Europe over the previous hundred years and more. It returned for a fourth time in 2014, with two hugely successful stages in Yorkshire and a third between Cambridge and London, including a sprint finish on The Mall.

*Giro d'Italia*

First run in 1908 to boost sales of the *La Gazzetta dello Sport* newspaper, the Giro follows the same general format as the Tour de France. The traditional finish is in Milan, where the GC winner is awarded the *maglia rosa* (pink jersey), pink being the colour of the pages of *La Gazzetta*.

Three riders have won the Giro five times:

- Alfredo Binda (Italy)

- Fausto Coppi (Italy)

- Eddy Merckx (Belgium)

Binda was the first Italian cycling superstar and he dominated the Giro in the 1920s. Gino Bartali, who was Coppi's great rival in the 1940s, holds the record for most King of the Mountains titles in the Giro (seven), with Robert Millar providing a solitary British win in 1987. Two Italians, Francesco Moser and Giuseppe Saronni, have won the sprinters' competition a record four times at the time of writing.

## No tourists were harmed in the running of this race

One of the most thrilling stages ever in the Giro was a time trial in 1978 that ran alongside the canals of Venice before finishing in the tourist trap of Piazza San Marco (St Mark's Square). It was won by legendary Italian sprinter and classics rider Francesco Moser.

---

### RE-CYCLED FACT

#### In nomine Patri...

It is traditional for the pope to bless the *maglia rosa* ahead of the Giro each year, and he will often also receive the riders at the start. Pope Pius XII made an exception in 1954 due to Fausto Coppi's very public marital indiscretions (adultery was still a criminal as well as a moral offence in Italy at the time). As a result, many of the Italian *tifosi* (fans) turned their backs on, or even spat at, Coppi during the ensuing race.

---

*Vuelta a España*

Established in 1935 to boost sales of the *Informaciones* newspaper, the Vuelta also follows the format of the Tour de France. Jersey colours have changed over the years but the GC winner is currently awarded the *jersey rojo* (red jersey) following the race's traditional finish in Madrid. Roberto Heras of Spain holds the record for most wins (four), achieved between 2000 and 2005. Ireland's Sean Kelly won it in 1988 and was the only rider from an English-speaking country to have done so until Chris Froome became the first British winner in 2017.

Kelly and France's Laurent Jalabert have been the Vuelta's top sprinters, having won four points classifications apiece.

The Spaniard José Luis Laguía has been the Vuelta's top climber, with a record five King of the Mountains titles in the 1980s.

Note: Roberto Heras was stripped of his fourth Vuelta win in 2005 after testing positive for EPO. After appealing the decision through the courts for the next seven years (on the grounds that his samples were mishandled and his test results inaccurate), he was eventually reinstated as 2005 champion in 2013, and awarded 724,000 euros compensation by the Spanish state in 2017.

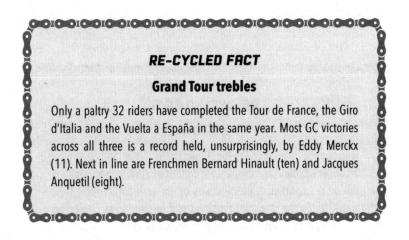

### RE-CYCLED FACT

### Grand Tour trebles

Only a paltry 32 riders have completed the Tour de France, the Giro d'Italia and the Vuelta a España in the same year. Most GC victories across all three is a record held, unsurprisingly, by Eddy Merckx (11). Next in line are Frenchmen Bernard Hinault (ten) and Jacques Anquetil (eight).

## Other Tours

*Tour Down Under*

First run in 1999, the Tour Down Under has already been promoted to the highest-ranking professional race outside Europe. Aside from the Tour de France, it also attracts the biggest crowds anywhere in the world – almost 800,000 over the six days of the event in and around Adelaide.

In order to save transportation costs for the international teams, this Tour has no time trials (which, of course, require different bikes and clothing), and as there are no hills worth speaking about in this part of South Australia, most stages will finish in a mass sprint. The biggest issue for the riders is the searing January heat. As of 2017, Aussie Simon Gerrans has won the Tour a record four times.

---

### RE-CYCLED FACT

#### Hero for a week

A wonderful tradition of the Tour Down Under is that the fans choose an unknown, non-English-speaking *domestique* (a rider who supports the more important team members by, for example, carrying their water during the race) and treat him as if he were a star. They mob him in hotels and paint his name on the roads on each day of the race.

---

*Paris–Nice*

First held in 1933, the week-long 'Race to the Sun' in March has normally finished with a mass sprint on the Promenade des Anglais, or on the nearby hill-climb of the Col d'Eze. The Irishman Sean Kelly has won the race the most times, with an astonishing seven consecutive wins between 1982 and 1988.

Briton Tom Simpson won the race in 1967, not long before the Tour de France that same year that would claim his life on Mont Ventoux in the French Alps. He remained the only Briton to have won the Paris–Nice classic until Bradley Wiggins achieved the feat in 2012, which Geraint Thomas followed up with a third British win in 2016.

## Critérium du Dauphiné

Run since 1947 in the first half of June over eight stages in the mountainous Dauphiné region of France, this is the last important race before the Tour de France each year. As such, it is used by many of the top riders to put the finishing touches to their Tour de France preparations. Five riders have won the classic three times as of 2017: Nello Lauredi, Charly Mottet, Bernard Hinault (all France), Luis Ocaña (Spain) and Chris Froome (Britain). Four Brits have now won the race: Brian Robinson in 1961, Robert Millar in 1990, Bradley Wiggins in 2011 and 2012, and Chris Froome in 2013, 2015 and 2016 (in all three of those years, he went on to win the Tour de France, so the preparation clearly worked a treat).

## Tour of Britain

Following previous incarnations that included the Milk Race and the Kellogg's Tour, the Tour of Britain is now an eight-day stage event held in September. In 2012, Jonathan Tiernan-Locke became the first Briton to win the Tour of Britain in its current form, and the first Briton to win any British tour since Chris Lillywhite won the Milk Race in 1993, but he was later disqualified for biological passport irregularities. Britain didn't have long to wait for another winner, though, as Bradley Wiggins won in 2013, and Steve Cummings notched up another British victory in 2016.

Mark Cavendish won the sprinters' points classification in 2007 and, as reigning World Road Race Champion, took three stage wins in 2012, including the final sprint on the final day up Guildford's cobbled High Street. He added three more stage wins the following year.

*Giro d'Italia Internazionale Femminile*

This eight-day stage race, nicknamed the *Giro Donne* ('women's tour'), is the only Grand Tour left in the women's calendar after lack of sponsorship saw the others fall by the wayside.

First raced in 1988, the Giro Donne has been won most times (five) by Italian rider Fabiana Luperini. Nicole Cooke is the only British rider to have won, in 2004, and Britain's Emma Pooley finished runner-up in 2011 and 2012, on both occasions to the top women's rider of recent years, the Dutchwoman Marianne Vos, who added a third Giro victory in 2014.

## Olympics (Road)

Different forms of individual and team road races came and went over the first hundred years of the modern Olympics, but since 1996 only individual road races and time trials have been held.

### World domination

Great Britain has at times punched way above its weight and only France has won more cycling medals in the entire history of the modern Olympics. GB won a record 36 cycling medals at the London 1908 games and again secured world domination a hundred years later in Beijing, with 25 medals, which it followed with 24 at London in 2012 and 12 at the Rio Games in 2016. Five of GB's six cycling gold medals at the Rio Games were won, either individually or as a team member, by Jason Kenny (three) and Laura Trott (two), who went on to consolidate their own slice of world domination by marrying one another the following month.

### Road race (men)

**Introduced**: Athens, Greece (1896)
**First winner**: Aristidis Konstantinidis (Greece)
**Most wins**: No multiple winners

**Other notable winners**: Fabio Casartelli (Italy)

**Fascinating facts**:

- The road cycling event in Athens in 1896 was an 87-km (54-mile) race to Marathon and back.

- Three years after winning his gold medal in Barcelona in 1992, Italian Fabio Casartelli lost his life after hitting his head on a concrete barrier on a mountain descent of the Tour de France.

- Bradley Wiggins, Chris Froome et al. were meant to deliver red-hot favourite Mark Cavendish to the front in time for him to sprint to glory in the 2012 race in London, but they lost out after getting caught in the pack while veteran Kazakh rider Alexandre Vinokourov snatched victory.

## Road race (women)

**Introduced**: Los Angeles, California, USA (1984)

**First winner**: Connie Carpenter (USA)

**Most wins**: No multiple winners

**Other notable winners**: Jeannie Longo (France); Nicole Cooke (GB); Marianne Vos (Netherlands)

**Fascinating fact**: Nicole Cooke's gold medal in Beijing in 2008 was GB's 200th in the modern Olympics.

## Time trial (men)

**Introduced**: Atlanta, Georgia, USA (1996)

**First winner**: Miguel Induráin (Spain)

**Most wins** (two): Viatcheslav Ekimov (Russia); Fabian Cancellara (Switzerland)

**Other notable winners**: Bradley Wiggins (GB)

**Fascinating facts**:

- The Russian Viatcheslav Ekimov won gold at Sydney in 2000 and at Athens in 2004, but he didn't receive his Athens gold until 2012, after the American Tyler Hamilton, who had been first over the line, finally confessed to doping throughout his career.
- Bradley Wiggins won his time-trial gold in 2012 at his home Olympics in London.

## Time trial (women)

**Introduced**: Atlanta, USA (1996)

**First winner**: Zulfiya Zabirova (Russia)

**Most wins** (three): Kristin Armstrong (USA)

**Fascinating facts**:

- Kristin Armstrong won time-trial gold at Beijing (2008), London (2012) and Rio (2016), despite being diagnosed with osteoarthritis in both hips in 2001 at the age of 27 and temporarily retiring to start a family in 2009. She became the oldest rider to win an Olympic time trial in 2012, a record she herself beat four years later in Rio on the day before her forty-third birthday.

- Dutch rider Leontien van Moorsel pulled out of professional cycling in 1994, suffering from anorexia, but recovered to resume one of the most successful cycling careers in history, including six Olympic medals. She won the time-trial gold in Sydney (2000) in addition to winning the women's road race, and again in Athens (2004), despite crashing in the road race just two days earlier.

## World Championships (road)

The World Championships are held annually at different venues around the world. The highlights of the week-long programme are the men's and women's single-stage road races and time trials.

### Road race (men)

**Introduced**: Nurbürgring, Germany (1927)

**First winner**: Alfredo Binda (Italy)

**Most wins** (three): Alfredo Binda (Italy); Óscar Freire (Spain); Eddy Merckx (Belgium), Rik van Steenbergen (Belgium); Peter Sagan (Slovakia)

**Other notable winners**: Fausto Coppi (Italy); Tom Simpson (GB); Bernard Hinault (France); Greg LeMond (USA); Stephen Roche (Ireland); Lance Armstrong (USA); Cadel Evans (Australia); Mark Cavendish (GB)

**Fascinating facts**:

- Tom Simpson won the race for Britain in San Sebastián in northern Spain in 1965, and remained the only British winner until Mark Cavendish finally repeated the feat in Copenhagen in 2011.

- Between them, Belgians and Italians have won well over half the gold medals on offer.

- Peter Sagan became the first winner of three consecutive championships when he won the 2017 race in Bergen, Norway.

### Road race (women)

**Introduced**: Reims, France (1958)

**First winner**: Elsy Jacobs (Luxembourg)

**Most wins** (five): Jeannie Longo (France)

**Other notable winners**: Nicole Cooke (GB); Marianne Vos (Netherlands); Lizzie Armitstead (now Deignan; GB)

**Fascinating facts**:

- Mandy Jones won for Great Britain at the age of 20 on home soil at Goodwood, West Sussex, in 1982. It was the only major win of her career.

- In 2008 Nicole Cooke became the first rider (male or female) to be World Road Race Champion and Olympic Road Race Champion in the same year.
- Dutch superstar Marianne Vos won gold in 2006 and 2012, and silver in each of the five years in between.

## Time trial (men)

**Introduced**: Agrigento/Catania, Italy (1994)

**First winner**: Chris Boardman (GB)

**Most wins** (four): Fabian Cancellara (Switzerland); Tony Martin (Germany)

**Other notable winners**: Miguel Induráin (Spain); Bradley Wiggins (GB)

**Fascinating facts**:

- Fabian Cancellara won his four gold medals in the space of five championships between 2006 and 2010, while Tony Martin won his four in the space of six championships between 2011 and 2016.
- Bradley Wiggins became the oldest winner of the race in 2014, at the age of 34 years 149 days.

## Time trial (women)

**Introduced**: Agrigento/Catania, Italy (1994)

**First winner**: Karen Kurreck (USA)

**Most wins** (four): Jeannie Longo (France)

**Other notable winners**: Emma Pooley (GB)

**Fascinating fact**: Emma Pooley won Britain's only gold medal to date in Melbourne in 2010.

### *RE-CYCLED FACT*

#### Over the rainbow

In common with other cycling disciplines, the Road Race and Time Trial World Champions wear the coveted 'rainbow jersey' for the whole of the year in which they reign. In fact, the jersey is predominantly white and contains only five colours in horizontal stripes – the same five colours as appear on the Olympic flag.

## Cycling at the Paralympic Games

Cycling became a Paralympic sport at the New York/Stoke Mandeville Games in 1984, and a handcycling programme was added at Athens in

2000. Road and track events now largely mirror those of the Olympics for all three disability groups (vision impaired, cerebral palsy and wheelchair), except that visually impaired sprinters ride on tandems so that they can have sighted guides.

Great Britain overtook Australia as the dominant force in Paralympic cycling at Beijing in 2008, and again topped the medal table at the London 2012 and Rio 2016 Games. British multiple medal winners include David Stone, Darren Kenny, Jody Cundy, Steve Bate and Sarah Storey (see Hall of Fame later for more information on Sarah Storey). The multi-talented Kadeena Cox won a cycling time-trial gold medal at Rio in addition to gold and bronze medals as a sprinter on the athletics track.

### *RE-CYCLED FACT*

#### The comeback king

The London 2012 Paralympic Games witnessed the astonishing feat of Italian former racing driver Alex Zanardi handbiking to two gold medals and a silver 11 years after losing both his legs following a horrific crash in an IndyCar race. He went on to win an identical haul of medals at the Rio Games in 2016.

# PART 2: TRACK

Here we will look at the unusual world of track cycling, focusing primarily on the five track events of the Olympic Games as currently constituted.

## Olympics (Track)

Different Olympic track events have come and gone since 1896, but they were finally standardised in 2012 for men and women as the keirin, omnium, team pursuit, individual sprint and team sprint.

*Keirin*

Japanese for 'racing wheels', the keirin started in Japan as a betting sport in 1948 and only became an Olympic event (for men) at Sydney in 2000. Riders stay in predetermined order behind a motorised pacer (known as a 'derny') until sprinting for victory over the last 600–700 metres at speeds of up to 43 mph (70 km/h). In 2012, Victoria Pendleton (GB) won the first-ever keirin for women in the Olympics and Chris Hoy (GB) successfully defended the title he had won in Beijing four years earlier. Jason Kenny took up where Chris Hoy left off to win the keirin gold in Rio.

*Omnium*

Consists of six sub-events:

- Flying lap (individually, against the clock).

- Points race: a mass-start multiple-lap race of 30 km for men and 20 km for women – points are awarded for intermediate sprints and for lapping other riders.

- Elimination race: sometimes referred to as 'devil take the hindmost', as the last rider to cross the line at the end of each lap (or a predetermined number of laps) is eliminated until the few remaining riders sprint to the finish.

- Individual pursuit: where two riders start on opposite sides of the track and race until they reach their respective finishing lines at the end of the race distance, or, in a final, until one catches the other (hence 'pursuit'). Was previously an event in its own right before being subsumed into the omnium in 2012.

- Scratch race: another mass-start multiple-lap race (15 km for men and 10 km for women), but results are determined on a simple first-past-the-post basis.

- Time trial: racing individually against the clock from a standing start over 1 km for men and 500 metres for women.

The Danish rider Lasse Norman Hansen won the inaugural men's event in 2012, while Laura Trott took gold for Britain in the inaugural women's competition and also won four years later in Rio.

*Team pursuit*

This is similar to the individual pursuit in the omnium, but with teams of four (men) or three (women) starting from opposite sides of the track. Teams ride in a line to minimise drag and take turns pacemaking at the front. Finishing time is when the front wheel of the third rider crosses the line, so it is not uncommon in the men's race for the fourth rider to take a 'death pull' at the front and then peel off exhausted while the remaining three sprint together for the line.

Great Britain won the men's event in 2008, 2012 and 2016. The Team GB women won the inaugural women's event in 2012, and followed that up with another gold in 2016.

*Individual sprint*

This is a one-against-one sprint, except the sprinting doesn't start until one of the riders breaks for the line at the end of the cat-and-mouse tactical game that precedes it on the banks of the velodrome. Frenchmen have won more gold medals (seven) than anyone else since its inception in 1896, though Chris Hoy (2008) and Jason Kenny (2012 and 2016) have both won for Britain in recent times. Introduced for women at Seoul in 1988, the event enjoyed epic battles over two Olympics between British rider Victoria Pendleton and her arch-rival, the Australian Anna Meares (Pendleton took gold in Beijing and Meares reversed the positions four years later in London).

## RE-CYCLED FACT

### Time out!

Nobody won the 1,000-metre sprint gold medal in 1908 after it was declared null and void because the four finalists (three British and one French) exceeded the time limit of 1 minute 45 seconds for the race. They had got so caught up in the cat-and-mouse tactical battle that they forgot to dash for the line.

The seemingly curious behaviour of the riders in the early stages of these races, as they vary speed between slow, 'nudging forward' and stationary (they balance the bike in a stationary position by converting the tension of their single-speed drivetrain into side-to-side motion), is designed to keep the opponent either in front (in order to benefit from an aerodynamic slipstream in the sprint) or higher up the velodrome bank (in order to force the opponent into a wider racing line).

*Team sprint*

The name is misleading, because this is a three-man or two-woman team time trial. It was introduced as a men's event in 2000 and as a women's event in 2012. In the case of the men's race, the first-lap pacemaker peels away at the end of that lap, the second-lap pacemaker does likewise at the end of the second lap and the third man sprints the final lap on his own. In the women's race, each rider must lead for one of the laps. In both cases, the two opposing teams race simultaneously, starting at opposite sides of the track as in a pursuit race. The men of Team GB took gold in Beijing, London and Rio.

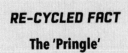

## RE-CYCLED FACT

### The 'Pringle'

The award-winning London 2012 velodrome was the first Olympic Park venue to be completed. Aerodynamic and energy-efficient, it was a triumph of engineering known affectionately as the 'Pringle' on account of its shape. Thirty-five miles (56 km) of Siberian pine and 350,000 nails were used in the construction of the 250-metre track.

## Clean sweep

Team GB won an impressive seven out of ten track cycling golds in Beijing in 2008 and London in 2012, and six out of the ten available in Rio in 2016. However, that was nothing compared to the statistics of the USA team in 1904. Only 18 track cyclists entered the games held in St Louis and they were all American. Over the course of the seven events held, the USA, rather unsurprisingly, took seven gold, seven silver and seven bronze. This is a record not likely to be beaten!

| Event | Gold | Silver | Bronze |
|-------|------|--------|--------|
| ¼ mile | USA | USA | USA |
| ⅓ mile | USA | USA | USA |

| ½ mile | USA | USA | USA |
|--------|-----|-----|-----|
| 1 mile | USA | USA | USA |
| 2 miles | USA | USA | USA |
| 5 miles | USA | USA | USA |
| 25 miles | USA | USA | USA |

## World Championships (Track)

Held annually at a different venue around the world, the format is very similar to that of the Olympics, except the time trial, individual pursuit, scratch and points events remain as individual competitions as well as being components of the omnium, and the men's Madison event (contested by up to 18 teams of two riders who take turns to race the intermediate sprints in which the points are won and lost) is alive and well.

The men's championships were inaugurated in Chicago in 1893, and the first women's events took place in Paris in 1958. France dominated the championships for a great many years, not least because they had a 14-times men's champion in Arnaud Tournant, and a 13-times women's champion in Jeannie Longo. In more recent years, with so many great cycling stars at its disposal, Great Britain has been one of the most competitive teams.

---

### *RE-CYCLED FACT*

#### Like waiting for a bus

In the 2013 World Championships in Minsk, Belarus, Martyn Irvine ended Ireland's 116-year wait for a medal, winning a silver in the individual pursuit. Ireland had to wait less than 116 years for its second medal, as Irvine returned an hour later to take gold in the scratch event (first past the post after 60 laps of the velodrome).

---

# PART 3: BMX

'BMX track' is a craze that swept 1970s America before becoming a World Championship event in 1982 and a full-blown Olympic event at Beijing in 2008. Riders bolt from a raised starting gate to race against one another for about 40 seconds on a rollercoaster of a course that includes wave-like bumps and berms (banked corners).

The USA leads the BMX World Championship medal table, and the magnificently named American Randy Stumpfhauser tops the men's individual medal table. The most successful women's rider is Gabriela Díaz of Argentina.

British rider Shanaze Reade won the women's BMX World Championship title three times (2007, 2008, 2010), while also finding time to partner Victoria Pendleton to World Championship gold (twice) and silver in the women's team sprint in the velodrome, a very different discipline to BMX track racing. British riders Dale Holmes (1996 and 2001) and Liam Phillips (2013) have both won the men's BMX World Championship.

Māris Štrombergs of Latvia became the first men's Olympic BMX champion in Beijing and successfully defended his title at London in 2012. Anne-Caroline Chausson of France became the first women's champion in Beijing, while Shanaze Reade, the reigning world champion at the time, fell in the final after clipping Chausson's rear wheel at the last turn. Mariana Pajón of Colombia, nicknamed the 'Queen of BMX', won gold at the London 2012 and Rio 2016 Games.

---

### BMX mongrel

The BMX bikes that were originally Schwinn Sting-Rays (see under 'BMX' in Chapter 2) were modified by swapping out the seat, handlebar, grips, forks, wheels, brakes and tyres, and then removing the fenders, kickstand, chain guard and reflectors. In other words, there wasn't much left of the Sting-Ray by the time it became a BMX, and even then it remained a bit heavy and clunky for the purpose of replicating motocross racing. Gary Turner (of GT Bicycles fame) was an aircraft and drag-racing welder who saw the inherent nonsense of this and designed the first production BMX in 1973.

---

## PART 4: MOUNTAIN BIKE

Like BMX track, mountain-bike racing is a young sport that kicked off in 1970s America. The first World Championships were held in 1990 in

Durango, Colorado, USA, and have been held once in the UK, at Fort William in Scotland, in 2007. The sport entered the Olympics at Atlanta in 1996.

Nerves of steel and bags of stamina are required to negotiate cross-country courses that entail rocky paths, tricky climbs and technical descents over an elapsed time of up to 2 hours. There are stations at designated points on the course for riders to make repairs to their bikes and take on much-needed sustenance.

Variations of the sport include downhill (an individual time trial), four-cross (downhill racing with four riders at a time) and trial riding (passing through urban obstacle courses without a foot touching the ground).

Let's have a closer look at the different disciplines which riders compete in at World Championship and Olympic level.

**Cross-country:** Nino Schurter (Switzerland) has won most men's cross-country world titles (six), and Gunn-Rita Dahle Flesjå of Norway tops the women's list with four wins. Cadel Evans, the first Australian winner of the Tour de France in 2010, won the Mountain Bike World Cup (which is a series event, different from the World Championship) in 1998 and 1999, and rode for Australia in the mountain bike event at the Sydney 2000 Olympics.

At the Olympics, Frenchman Julien Absalon has won two men's gold medals (Athens 2004 and Beijing 2008) and Italian rider Paola Pezzo has won two women's titles (Atlanta 1996 and Sydney 2000). The London 2012 cross-country venue was at Hadleigh Farm in Essex, on land owned by the Salvation Army. Julie Bresset of France won the women's race, and Jaroslav Kulhavý of the Czech Republic won the men's after a thrilling sprint finish with Nino Schurter. Schurter got his revenge when the placings were reversed in Rio four years later, a race in which Slovakian road-racing superstar Peter Sagan also featured until suffering a puncture on the second lap.

**Downhill:** Frenchman Nicolas Vouilloz reigns supreme in the World Championship downhill list, with seven world titles in eight years between 1995 and 2002. Vouilloz's compatriot, Anne-Caroline Chausson, did even better, winning nine women's titles in ten years between 1996 and 2005. As we have already seen, she also went on to win the first-ever BMX track gold medal at the Beijing Olympics in 2008. Britain has produced three men's downhill world champions: Gee Atherton (2008 and 2014), Steve Peat (2009) and Danny Hart (2011 and 2016); and three women's downhill champions: four-times winner Rachel Atherton (2008, 2013, 2015 and 2016), Tracy Moseley (2010) and Manon Carpenter (2014).

**Four-cross:** American Brian Lopes (2002, 2005 and 2007) and Czech Michal Prokop (2003, 2006 and 2011) each won the men's World Championship three times. Aussie rider Caroline Buchanan has won the Women's World Championship five times between 2009 and 2017, while Katy Curd became the first British winner in 2014.

**Trials:** There are two separate events for the men, the 20-inch trials and the 26-inch trials, whereas the women compete in only one (26-inch) discipline (just in case you don't know, we're talking wheel size here). Spaniard Benito Ros reigned supreme in the 20-inch event by winning ten out of twelve World Championships between 2003 and 2014, while French rider Gilles Coustellier won five 26-inch championships between 2008 and 2014. Jack Carthy became the first British winner of a Trials

World Championship (the 26-inch event) in 2016. Swiss rider Karin Moor won nine of the first eleven Women's Trials between 2001and 2011.

---

### The godfather of mountain biking

We have already seen how Gary Fisher's name became synonymous with the mountain bike, as he is considered to be one of its inventors. He himself started competing in road and track races in 1963 at the age of 12, but was suspended from racing as a 17-year-old for having long hair and it was four years before the daft rule was repealed. He went on to win races that included the brutal TransAlp Challenge, the original epic mountain bike race in Europe (still run annually over eight gruelling days), and in 1977 he set the record of 4 minutes 22 seconds on the infamous Repack Downhill, a tortuous descent of 1,300 feet over 2 miles (400 metres in 3.2 km) in Fairfax, California.

---

## PART 5: CYCLO-CROSS

A winter sport that consists of laps of a cross-country track, with races lasting for about an hour. Cyclo-cross differs from mountain-bike racing in that riders have to cross obstacles that require dismounting and the carrying of bikes over their shoulders (normally for about 5 per cent of the race). Aerobic endurance and bike-handling skills are of the essence.

Cyclo-cross is thought to have originated in France and Belgium in the early 1900s as riders raced each other to the next town over roads, through fields, across streams and over hedges or fences. These men were referred to as *coureurs de steeple* ('steeplechasers') because a church steeple was often all they had to aim for while the rest of the town in question remained below the horizon.

The sport grew slowly but surely until the first World Championships were held in Paris in 1950. It then took off in America at the same time as BMX and mountain biking did in the 1970s, but the championships never left mainland Europe – until 2013, when they finally made it across the Atlantic to Louisville, Kentucky.

The Belgian Erik de Vlaeminck has won most gold medals in the men's competition, with seven titles between 1966 and 1973. The women's World Championships were inaugurated in 2000 and were won seven times in nine years, between 2006 and 2014, by Dutch super-rider Marianne Vos.

One of the longest and hardest cyclo-cross races in the world is the Three Peaks Cyclo-cross, which has been run in Yorkshire since 1961. Local runner Rob Jebb has dominated the men's race in the twenty-first century, and Louise Robinson (daughter of Brian Robinson, the first Briton to win a stage of the Tour de France in 1958) has won the women's race a record five times.

### Merry Veldrijden

Literally 'field-riding', *veldrijden* is Flemish for cyclo-cross and the Belgians of the Flanders region in particular go mad for it. And I don't just mean the riders who compete at everything from junior to elite level; I mean also the hordes of spectators who turn out in all conditions to watch the 'weekend warriors' battle through mud, snow and ice. Even Christmas Day is an important fixture in the world of *veldrijden*.

# PART 6: CYCLE SPEEDWAY

Four riders race individual and team events over four laps around an oval track. Physical contact is legal and often necessary to stay on the bike or get the better of an opponent.

Similar in format to motorcycle speedway, the cycle version is said to have taken off in post-war Britain as a way for youngsters with not much else to do to enjoy themselves. They cleared tracks through the rubble of bomb sites and used bikes that were not otherwise roadworthy. Within five years there were about 200 clubs in East London alone and the sport had spread around the country.

After it had found its way to the Netherlands, an international between that country and England in 1950 at Earls Court attracted 10,000 spectators. But, as bomb sites were cleared for fresh building and young men were drafted for national service, the sport fell away, but never entirely.

Resurrected in the 1970s, the sport has since grown internationally and now includes Russia, the USA and Australia. Men's World Championships have been held since 1958 and Great Britain has produced nine champions, including three-times winner Dave Hemsley, and Jim Varnish, father of

Olympic track sprinter Jess Varnish. Laura Watson took the inaugural women's World Championship for Britain in 2011, 2 seconds ahead of fellow Sheffield cyclist Vicky Brown, and Lauren Davies kept the British flag flying high with victory in 2013.

Many cycle speedway riders go on to other disciplines, most notably Australian Brett Aitken, who went on to win gold, silver and bronze Olympic track-cycling medals for his country.

# PART 7: HALL OF FAME

The list of multiple-race-winning cyclists is a long one, so the following 'Hall of Fame' celebrates the achievements of just a few of those who have succeeded more than once, more often than not over a long number of years, and very often across more than one cycling discipline.

## Great British cyclists

Britain has punched way above its weight in recent times, producing many of the best riders the world has ever seen. Here are some of the major achievers over the last 25 years or so.

---

### Chris Hoy

**Born**: 1976, Edinburgh, Scotland
**Discipline**: Track (keirin, sprint, time trial)

---

**Nickname**: The Real McHoy

Along with Jason Kenny (see next entry), Chris Hoy is the joint most successful Olympic cyclist in history, and the joint most successful British Olympian of all time, with six gold medals and one silver. In the track events he specialised in (sprint, time trial and keirin), the Edinburgh-born rider also amassed 11 World Championship titles. As BBC Sports Personality of the Year 2008, he was only the second cyclist ever to win the award (43 years after Tom Simpson had won it in 1965). Knighted in the 2009 New Year Honours List and immortalised in the Sir Chris Hoy Velodrome built for the 2014 Commonwealth Games in Glasgow.

## Jason Kenny

**Born**: 1988, Farnworth, Greater Manchester

**Discipline**: Track (sprint, keirin)

After dabbling in football (as a goalkeeper), cricket and tennis while growing up (his PE teachers knew he had something special, they just didn't know what exactly), Kenny won his first Olympic gold cycling medal in Beijing at the age of just 20.

By 2016, he had joined Chris Hoy as one of the two most successful Olympic cyclists in history after equalling Hoy's record of six Olympic gold medals and one silver. Kenny has won his medals over three Olympic Games (Beijing, London and Rio) and has also won three World Championships.

He was awarded an MBE in 2009, an OBE in 2013 and a CBE in 2017.

## Laura Trott (now Kenny)

**Born**: 1992, Harlow, Essex

**Discipline**: Track (team pursuit, omnium, scratch)

**Nickname**: Trotty

Having been born with a collapsed lung and later diagnosed as asthmatic, Laura Trott was advised to take up some sport or other to help regulate her breathing. She tried trampolining, but it didn't work, and she later took up cycling alongside her mother, who was trying to lose weight at the time. Having won omnium and team pursuit gold medals at both the London 2012 and Rio 2016 Games, she became the most successful female track cyclist in Olympic history and Britain's most successful Olympic female competitor in any sport. She has also amassed seven World Championship victories and a record ten European Championship wins, plus a Commonwealth Games gold medal while recovering from a kidney infection.

She was awarded an OBE in 2013 and a CBE in 2017, and the Laura Trott Leisure Centre in Cheshunt, Hertfordshire, is named in her honour.

## Bradley Wiggins

**Born**: 1980, Ghent, Belgium

**Discipline**: Track (Madison, pursuit) and road

**Nickname**: Wiggo

A rare breed of cyclist who has enjoyed success on the track and on the road, Wiggins is a cycling legend who took to track cycling after watching Chris Boardman win gold at the 1992 Barcelona Olympics. He has won four Olympic track gold medals, plus six World Championship track titles.

Having made the difficult switch to road racing, Wiggins swept all before him in 2012, winning the Paris–Nice, the Tour de Romandie, the Critérium du Dauphiné, the Tour de France (as the first-ever British winner of the race) and the Olympic road time trial. This unprecedented level of success brought him the BBC Sports Personality of the Year award for 2012 and a knighthood in the 2013 New Year Honours List.

He is the only rider to win Olympic and World Championship titles on both the road and the track, and his other outstanding achievements include holding the hour record on the track and the leader's jersey in each of the three Grand Tours on the road. With five gold, one silver and two bronze, he has also at the time of writing won more Olympic medals than any other British Olympian in history.

Away from cycling, Wiggins is an enthusiastic musician and well-known follower of the mod style that kicked off in the sixties, so he got a real thrill out of playing guitar at a charity concert with fellow mod Paul Weller in 2012. Since retiring from cycling in 2016, he has taken up rowing and hopes to compete in the discipline at national and international level.

## Mark Cavendish

**Born**: 1985, Douglas, Isle of Man

**Discipline**: Road and track (Madison, points, scratch)

**Nickname**: The Manx Missile

The 'Manx Missile' is the fastest road sprinter ever, having earlier cut his teeth on the track with two world titles in the Madison in 2005 and 2008. He returned to the track in 2016 to win a third Madison world title and again at the 2016 Rio Olympic Games to win a silver medal in the omnium event.

The explosive bursts of speed that propel him to the finishing line in road races have already resulted in 30 Tour de France stage wins at the time of writing – only Eddy Merckx has won more (34), but nobody has won more in terms of mass-finish sprints alone. In 2008, Cavendish took two sprint stages in the Giro and four in the Tour at the age of just 23. He blasted his way to six more Tour stage wins in 2009 alone. In 2011, he became the first-ever British winner of the Tour de France green jersey, and in the same year ended Britain's 46-year wait for a road race world champion. He won the BBC Sports Personality of the Year trophy in 2011, with an astonishing 49 per cent of the public vote, and was also awarded an MBE. In 2012, he became the first rider to win the final stage of the Tour de France on the Champs-Élysées in four consecutive years. Another proud moment came when he won the first (sprint) stage of the 2016 Tour de France and thereby earned the right to wear the coveted yellow jersey the following day.

## Chris Froome

**Born**: 1985, Nairobi, Kenya

**Discipline**: Road

**Nickname**: Froomey

After competing for Kenya in the 2006 Commonwealth Games in Melbourne, Froome started riding under a British licence in 2008 and represented England in the 2010 Commonwealth Games in Delhi. As a professional, he broke through as a contender by finishing second in the 2011 Vuelta and winning his first Tour de France stage in 2012 while helping Bradley Wiggins to victory within Team Sky. He then joined the greats of the cycling world by winning the Tour in four out of the next five years (2013, 2015, 2016 and 2017) and may yet add more. His winning Tour de France sequence was interrupted by retirement following multiple crashes in the 2014 race. In 2017, he finally won the Vuelta, becoming the first Briton to win a major Tour other than the Tour de France and the first rider to win the Tour–Vuelta double since 1978. He has also won two Olympic bronze medals, in the time-trial event at the London 2012 and Rio 2016 Games.

He was awarded the OBE in 2016 and is an ambassador for wildlife conservation, sporting a rhino graphic on the top tube of his bikes to highlight the plight of that particular animal.

## Chris Boardman

**Born**: 1968, Hoylake, Merseyside

**Discipline**: Road and track (pursuit)

**Nicknames**: The Professor, Mr Prologue

The engaging British rider, now a popular TV presenter, won the individual-pursuit track gold medal at the Barcelona Olympics in 1992, and went on to become a world champion in both track pursuit (twice) and road time trial.

He won a total of three Tour de France prologue time trials (Lille in 1994, Rouen in 1997 and Dublin in 1998) and, because prologues always take place on day one of the Tour, these wins guaranteed that he got to wear the coveted *maillot jaune* in three separate years. He recorded the fastest time trial in history in 1994, when he completed the Lille prologue course at an average speed of 55.152 km/h (34.270 mph), and he set the world hour record on three separate occasions.

Somewhat bizarrely, and quite appropriately given his propensity to eat them up, his middle name is Miles.

## Lizzie Armitstead (now Deignan)

**Born**: 1988, Otley, West Yorkshire

**Discipline**: Road and track (team pursuit, scratch, points)

**Nickname**: Elizabeth the First

Lizzie Armitstead came to prominence as a track cyclist at the 2009 World Championships. Having won gold in the team pursuit, she won silver in the scratch race in spite of being brought down in the closing stages, and then bronze in the points race with her right wrist bandaged up as a result of her fall in the scratch event.

Having switched to road racing, she won the first of four National Road Race Championships to date in 2011. She was nicknamed 'Elizabeth the First' by the British media in 2012 after winning the first Team GB medal of the home Olympic Games in London, finishing second behind Marianne Vos in the road race event. Road-racing gold medals would soon follow, though, with individual victories in the 2014 Commonwealth Games (just one week after crashing on the Champs-Élysées in the final stretch of La Course by Le Tour de France) and 2015 World Championships, followed by a time-trial team gold at the 2016 World Championships.

## Victoria Pendleton

**Born**: 1980, Stotfold, Bedfordshire

**Discipline**: Road and track (sprint, team sprint, keirin)

**Nickname**: Queen Victoria

Victoria Pendleton is one of Britain's most successful female Olympians, with two gold medals and one silver. She won the individual sprint in Beijing in 2008 and took gold in the keirin and silver in the individual sprint at the London 2012 Games. She also won nine world titles, including a record six in the individual sprint between 2005 and 2012, as well as two golds at the European Championships and one at the Commonwealth Games.

She was awarded the MBE in 2009 and the CBE in 2013. Following her retirement from cycling, she appeared as a contestant on *Strictly Come Dancing* and then got back in the saddle in 2015, but this time as a jockey. She won her first race in 2016, just before finishing a very creditable fifth in the 2016 Foxhunter Chase at Cheltenham.

## Geraint Thomas

**Born**: 1986, Cardiff, Wales

**Discipline**: Road and track (team pursuit, individual pursuit)

**Nickname**: G

Geraint Thomas has a fearless riding style that has brought him much success on the track and the road, but it has also brought him a fair share of crashes and injuries (including a ruptured spleen, broken pelvis, fractured nose and broken collarbone). As a member of the British pursuit team on the track, he has won two Olympic and three World Championship gold medals. On the road, he has won the British National Road Race Championships plus a Commonwealth Games gold medal for Wales (in spite of having to change a wheel in the closing stages). He completed his first Tour de France at the age of just 21.

As a founder member of Team Sky, Thomas has played a significant part in Chris Froome's Tour victories as well as winning the opening stage of the 2017 Tour himself, becoming the first Welshman ever to wear the yellow jersey, although he later crashed out of the race with a broken collarbone. His other individual successes have included winning the sprinter classification in the 2013 Tour Down Under, plus outright victories in the 2016 Paris–Nice and 2017 Tour of the Alps stage races.

He was awarded the MBE in 2009.

## Sarah Storey

**Born**: 1977, Manchester

**Discipline**: Road and track (pursuit and time trial)

I complete my British 'Hall of Fame' with a remarkable British Paralympian who was born without a functioning left hand, but who went on to win five gold, eight silver and three bronze Paralympic swimming medals before switching to cycling for the Beijing Paralympics in 2008. Storey won two cycling golds in Beijing, four more in London in 2012 and three more again in Rio in 2016, making a staggering total of 25 Paralympic medals to date, including 14 golds, making her the most successful British female Paralympian of all time.

She has won national track titles against non-disabled cyclists and has similarly represented England at the Commonwealth Games against able-bodied athletes. She was awarded the MBE in 1998 and the OBE in 2009, before being made a dame in the 2013 New Year Honours List.

## Young guns

In 2016, 23-year-old Adam Yates became the first British cyclist to win the Tour de France white jersey in the Best Young Rider classification, while finishing fourth overall in the race. He had previously won the 2014 Tour of Turkey and the 2015 Clásica de San Sebastián.

In 2017, Simon Yates, twin brother of Adam, became the second British cyclist to win the Tour de France white jersey in the Best Young Rider classification, while finishing seventh overall in the race. The year before, he had won a stage in the Vuelta, the first of the twins to win a Grand Tour stage victory.

When Simon stepped onto the podium for the first time to take the white jersey in the Tour de France, the hostess in the white dress (Tour de France hostesses always wear dresses that match the jersey being awarded) said: 'Nice to see you again', clearly mistaking him for Adam from the year before.

## Other great cyclists

Britain has not always had its own way, of course. Here are just half a dozen of the best non-Brits to have ridden into greatness over the years.

### Eddy Merckx

**Born**: 1945, Meensel-Kiezegem, Belgium
**Discipline**: Road

**Nickname**: The Cannibal

Widely regarded to be the greatest rider of all time, Merckx lived up to his nickname of 'the Cannibal' in the 1960s and 1970s by gobbling up kilometres, trophies and records in a way that is unlikely ever to be surpassed. During his astonishing career he won the Tour de France and the Giro d'Italia five times each, three World Championships and one Vuelta a España. He is one of only two riders (along with Stephen Roche of Ireland) to win cycling's Triple Crown by winning the Tour, the Giro and the World Championship in the same year (1974). He also won all five of the Monument classics at least twice each.

In 1996, the King of Belgium awarded him the ceremonial title of 'Baron', and in 2000 he was chosen as Belgium's Sports Figure of the Century.

## Marianne Vos

**Born**: 1987, 's-Hertogenbosch, the Netherlands

**Discipline**: Road, track (points, scratch, Madison), cyclo-cross, mountain biking

**Nickname**: *Vosje* ('Little Fox')

An unstoppable force in women's racing, the Dutch superwoman has won 12 world titles across three different cycling disciplines: road (three times), track (twice) and cyclo-cross (seven times). Having already been Dutch junior mountain bike champion (four times) and Dutch junior road race champion (twice), she became road-race world champion and cyclo-cross world champion in 2006, aged just 19, and added her first track World Championship two years later. She then added Olympic track gold in Beijing in 2008.

In 2012, she surpassed even her own ridiculously high standards, winning the Olympic road race, the World Championship road race, the Giro d'Italia Femminile and three World Cup races in a single year. As the dominant force in women's road racing, she ended that year as world number one in the UCI rankings by a long way.

## Fabian Cancellara

**Born**: 1981, Wohlen bei Bern, Switzerland

**Discipline**: Road

**Nickname**: Spartacus

Nicknamed 'Spartacus' on account of his fighting spirit, the Swiss rider achieved phenomenal success as a time triallist and as a classics specialist. As a time triallist, he is a four-times world champion. He won the opening stage of the Tour de France five times, and wore the yellow jersey for 28 days in total, which is a record for any rider who hasn't won the Tour. He also won Olympic time-trial gold in 2008 in Beijing. As a classics rider, he won Paris–Roubaix three times, the Tour of Flanders three times and the Milan–San Remo once.

## Jeannie Longo

**Born**: 1958, Annecy, France

**Discipline**: Road, track, mountain biking

**Nickname**: The Cannibal

The appropriately named French rider competed long and hard across a staggering seven Olympic Games, winning four medals, including one gold. At her final Olympics in Beijing in 2008, she missed out on a fifth medal by 2 seconds, notwithstanding that many of her fellow competitors had not been born when she raced in her first Olympics in Los Angeles in 1984. She was world road race champion five times, road time-trial world champion four times and a track world champion on four occasions. She achieved the women's world hour record in 2000 in Mexico City, and proved her versatility yet further by winning silver in 1993 in the Mountain Bike and Trials World Championships.

Longo has often been acclaimed as the female equivalent of the great Eddy Merckx, hence the shared nickname.

## Sean Kelly

**Born**: 1956, Carrick-on-Suir, Ireland

**Discipline**: Road

**Nickname**: King Kelly

Irish rider Sean Kelly didn't just win four green jersey competitions at the Tour de France; he was one of the most successful riders of the 1980s and one of the great classics winners of all time, winning a total of nine Monuments. As we have seen, he also won the Paris–Nice stage race a staggering seven years in a row. He was the first rider to be ranked number one when world rankings were introduced to cycling in 1984, a position he held on to for a record-breaking six years.

## Peter Sagan

**Born**: 1990, Žilina, Slovakia

**Discipline**: Road, cyclo-cross, mountain bike

**Nicknames**: Peter the Great, The Terminator

Peter Sagan is a man who knows how to handle a bike. He started winning mountain-bike and cyclo-cross races as a youngster, becoming the junior MTB cross-country world champion at the age of 18. He once turned up for a Slovak Cup race in tennis shoes, shorts and a T-shirt and riding a supermarket bike with dodgy brakes borrowed from his sister – and won, despite being up against older competitors.

Having converted to road racing, he immediately started winning stages and sprinter classifications, including three stages in his first Grand Tour, the 2011 Vuelta. In his first Tour de France in 2012, at the age of 22, he won his very first stage (the first of three stage wins that year) and the green jersey for topping the sprinters' points classification – he also won a Porsche after betting his team's president that he could win two stages and the green jersey at the first time of asking.

At the time of writing, Sagan has now won 12 Grand Tour stages and five Tour de France green jerseys. His other achievements include winning three consecutive World Road Race Championships (2015–2017), becoming the first man in history to do so, and the 2016 Tour of Flanders.

A great personality who lights up every race and post-race interview he attends, Sagan is also known for his flamboyant victory poses when crossing the finishing line.

# CHAPTER 7

# *IN TRAINING*

*There is something wrong with a society that drives a car to a workout in the gym.*

Bill Nye, American science educator and comedian
(popularly known as 'Bill Nye, the Science Guy')

Many people cycle to keep fit and healthy, or in the hope of shedding a few pounds. If you are one of those people, you have chosen a remarkably clever option, because the bike absorbs a lot of the punishment your poor bones would have to take if you had chosen, say, running instead. On a bike, you get to enjoy the ride while simultaneously reaping the benefits of the exercise.

If, however, you want to cycle at a serious, even competitive, level, then you need to accept you are going to have to make your body suffer a bit in order to achieve your touring or racing goals. In which case, you might want to read up on the kind of training and nutrition that will help you achieve your ideal riding weight, which will bring you to the right amount of fitness at the right time and will aid your recovery from the rigours of long journeys or racing, or even from strain and injury.

You might look at photographs of the early cycling stars on the continent, with cigarettes hanging from their mouths and a hip flask of brandy in their back pockets, and conclude that all this modern sports science is really for wimps. But it's there, so you might as well use it.

## TRAINING REGIME

If you're a top professional rider, all you have to do is turn up and do as you're told whenever you're summoned to the team camp – complete with trainers, nutritionists, chefs and masseurs – and make sure you're not late for your session in the gym, altitude centre or wind tunnel.

If you're not, devise a training plan with the help of someone who understands the type of training you need for the kind of racing or touring you want to do. This might involve:

- Getting advice on your ideal riding/racing position.

- Building up from low-intensity workouts in the gym.

- A strength and conditioning programme to develop the core muscles that cycling alone can't reach.

- Putting in the miles on the road to maximise your aerobic and anaerobic capacities (the anaerobic system enables your muscles to recover in time for the next burst of speed or mountainside breakaway).

- Maintaining a positive attitude, because the right frame of mind plus a strong injection of will power will allow you to achieve more than you ever thought possible.

- If you're getting serious, training at altitude – ride up and down mountains during the day but make sure you sleep at the top at night.

- If you're getting really serious, finding a sports psychologist to tell you that you're unbeatable in heaven and on earth.

---

### RE-CYCLED FACT

#### Winter sun

Italy, Malta, Portugal, Cyprus and Spain, including the Canary Islands and Mallorca, are among the destinations that can provide you with warm-weather training camps if you need to escape the northern European cold and ice in winter. Sky Pro Cycling use Mallorca, so that obviously works.

---

You might also consider creating your own indoor training regime. Simply purchase a 24-gear digital-console training bike with automatic tilt mechanism and use the software supplied to create your own 'authentic' routes in the French Alps or Canadian Rockies. Feel every incline and decline as if you were there and feel just the right amount of wind thanks to the 'intelligent wind resistance' you have factored in according to your own height, weight and riding-style profiles.

## *NUTRITION*

There is no shortage of books or online advice on healthy nutrition, or on the types of food and drink that are particularly suited to different types of exercise or training. You might also want to ascertain during your training sessions how your body reacts to different pre-race food and drink types (legal stimulants such as caffeine can offer a nice jolt if taken before a race, but not if you've discovered during training that it makes you jittery or anxious for a couple of hours), and which in-race foods and drinks give you the greatest boost.

Whatever your personal foibles and requirements might be, you have to understand the basic fact that carbohydrates provide you with glucose, which you need to fuel your muscles, which you need to make your pedals turn (you probably knew that last bit anyway). Fats and proteins will also convert to glucose, but over a much longer period, and you'll probably have bonked by the time a Mars bar gets round to fuelling your muscles, so stick to carbs.

Because it's extremely difficult to eat a bowl of spaghetti bolognese during a race, however, you need to find other ways of taking on carbs. Dried fruit, sports drinks and energy bars are excellent choices, as are the energy gels that you see the top racers slugging at regular intervals.

So here is a handy summary of the golden rules to follow if you're racing or touring over long distances:

---

### Golden rules on the go

................................................................................

- Eat before you're hungry.

- Drink before you're thirsty.

- Take carbs every 30 minutes.

- Don't try to eat a bowl of pasta on your bike (especially not on a downhill section of the race).

- Always wash down your carbs (especially energy gels, which will otherwise sit like gooey sludge in the pit of your stomach).

- Practise eating food on your bike beforehand (it's very frustrating to keep dropping it somewhere between the back pocket of your jersey and your mouth).

---

## Recovery foods

If you're at the serious end of the scale, you also need to understand the foodstuffs that will aid recovery from rigorous or long-term touring or riding, or from different types of injury. Proteins, vitamins, minerals and antioxidants help heal wounds, mend bones, and 'de-stress' tendons. Here are some examples:

- Carrots, spinach and sweet potatoes are good for 'road rash', as they contain vitamin A, which helps create the white blood cells essential for warding off the infection that can come from flesh wounds.

- Oranges, strawberries, peppers and broccoli will help repair tissues and cartilage by increasing collagen levels, an essential protein in the rebuilding of scar tissue, blood vessels and bone cells.

- Turkey, chicken, fish and sirloin steak are especially good for the concentrated protein that athletes need to recover quickly from injury – the last thing you want to do during the early stages of an injury, therefore, is reduce your protein intake because you think you need to compensate for a reduced level of exercise.

- Milk and yoghurt contain the calcium that you need to repair injured muscle and bone, and also provide the vitamin D that improves calcium absorption, which in turn accelerates the repair process.

- Cereals provide the levels of zinc that are known to boost the immune system and heal wounds, and also give you the carbohydrates that prevent your system from dipping into protein for energy, thereby leaving your protein free to undertake repairs.

- Salmon, tuna and trout are packed with the omega-3 fatty acids, which quench inflammation, the natural enemy of recovery from tendonitis, bone fractures and sprained ligaments. Anti-inflammatory drugs like ibuprofen can be surprisingly counterproductive in this respect, as they are said to overdo the quenching and you do apparently need some residual inflammation to aid the healing process.

In the next chapter, we will look at nutrition in more detail for regular cyclists who are not looking to win Grand Tour road stages or Olympic events.

## Take it to the (VO$_2$) max

VO$_2$ max may sound like shampoo to the uninitiated, but to the trained endurance athlete it means maximal oxygen consumption, or maximal aerobic capacity (V = volume, O$_2$ = oxygen and max = maximum). VO$_2$ max is reached when oxygen consumption remains at a steady rate notwithstanding an increased work rate, and can be expressed as millilitres of oxygen per kilogram of body weight per minute (ml/kg/min). To give you an idea of what this means in English, consider the following (very rough) statistics, expressed as ml/kg/min, for average-sized people in their 'athletic prime':

| | |
|---|---|
| **Sedentary healthy female** | 35–40 |
| **Sedentary healthy male** | 40–45 |
| **Regular male cyclist** | 50–60 |
| **Professional male road racer** | 70–80 |
| **Top cross-country skier** | 80–90 |

There are plenty of exceptions to all of those very rough statistics, and the professional bike racers who have enjoyed the VO$_2$ levels of top cross-country skiers include five-times Tour de France winner Miguel Induráin of Spain (with a VO$_2$ of 88) and three-times Tour de France winner American Greg LeMond (with a staggering 92.5). That aerobic capacity may have had something to do with them winning the Tour de France on multiple occasions!

And, finally, here are some rough statistics about the calories we are all so obsessed about burning in the twenty-first century (these ones are based on one hour of activity by a person weighing 59 kg (9 st. 4 lb):

| Playing the cello | 118 |
|---|---|
| Leisure cycling | 236 |
| Unicycling | 295 |
| Mountain biking | 502 |
| Road racing | 708 |

So if mountain biking isn't your thing, try playing two cellos on a unicycle for an hour – it's pretty much the same thing in terms of staying fit and healthy.

# CHAPTER 8

# BICYCLE AND RIDER MAINTENANCE

*The bicycle has a soul. If you love it, it will give you emotions that you will never forget.*

Mario Cipollini, Italian sprinter who won 191 professional races

It is important to maintain your bike in good working order and to know at least the basics when it comes to fixing problems on the go. It is even more important to keep yourself in good working order, so in this chapter we'll look at maintaining both your bike and yourself and include some tips on how to improve your cycling performance.

## BIKE MAINTENANCE

Ideally, you should rent or buy accommodation next door to a bike-repair shop and never go cycling without a relative or friend who knows how to fix stuff. Let's assume, though, that you've been careless enough to live miles from your nearest bike-repair shop and that you sometimes go cycling on your own.

You're going to have to carry a puncture-repair kit, a spare tube, a bicycle multi-tool and a pump or $CO_2$ inflator when you're out and about, and you should invest in a bike-repair book or check out online help options if you want to dabble as a grease monkey at home. The DIY option is becoming increasingly beneficial as more and more people take up cycling without a commensurate increase in bike mechanics – these days, many of the larger stores won't service bikes they haven't sold themselves because they simply don't have the resources to do so.

Here are some handy tips that might come in useful if you're a new, occasional or rusty cyclist.

## Repair a puncture

Let's start with what is for many the most feared problem that can beset us in the middle of nowhere – the dreaded puncture. The best thing to do with a puncture is not to get one in the first place, so make sure you always check your tyre pressures are correct before every ride and check your tyres regularly for wear and tear and for anything that might have lodged in the rubber (like a nail). Assuming you've done all that and you're still unlucky enough to get a puncture, here's how to set about mending it:

- Turn the bike upside down and remove the wheel that has the flat tyre (most bikes now have a quick-release handle to get the wheel off easily). If the flat is on the back wheel, you might want to shift your chain down to the smallest gear, which will put it in a straight line and give it more slack, making it easier to remove and replace the wheel.

- Starting at the opposite side of the wheel from the valve position, insert the thin end of a tyre lever between the tyre and the wheel rim.

- Pull the lever down and clip the hook end of the lever to the nearest spoke.

- Move round two spokes and repeat the process with your second tyre lever, then alternate the levers until one side of the tyre is off the rim.

- Pull the other wall of the tyre off the rim with your hands.

- Remove the old tube from inside the tyre.

- Unless the object that caused the puncture is obvious on the outside of the tyre, run your hand around the inside of the tyre to find the offending matter. Either way, push the object back through with the flat of your tyre lever. Do all this gently to avoid extending the tyre puncture into your flesh.

- Pump a couple of strokes of air into the new tube (unless you don't have one and you're competent enough to repair the puncture in the old tube, in which case go right ahead and then pump some air into the repaired tube).

- Starting by inserting the valve of the tube through the hole in the rim, put the whole tube inside the tyre.

- Working around the wheel with your hands from the point nearest the valve, push one side of the tyre onto the rim.

- Check that there is no piece of tube pinched between the tyre and the rim and pull it back inside if there is.

- Again, starting from the point nearest the valve, push the other side of the tyre onto the wheel rim with your thumbs, with an extra bit of pressure required towards the end of the circle as the tyre becomes taut.

- Use your pump to inflate the tube to about half the pressure recommended on the wall of the tyre. Give the wheel a spin and check to see if the tyre is sitting evenly on the wheel. If not, deflate the tube and re-seat the tyre. Once you are satisfied that the tyre is sitting evenly, inflate the tube the whole way.

- Put the wheel back on the bike and make sure you turn the quick-release handle fully back to the 'closed' position.

- Pat yourself on the back, put your tools away in your saddlebag and cycle off, whistling in a carefree manner as you go.

### General maintenance

Look after your bike to keep it rolling smoothly and to prolong its active life. Here are the essential rules that you should always abide by:

- **Clean your bike regularly:** when your bike looks as if it is due a good clean, or at least every month in any event, turn it upside down or put it up on a stand to get to the difficult-to-reach parts and use a general bike cleaner. If you wipe your bike down quickly after each ride, you will find that the monthly clean is much less onerous. Cleaning your bike regularly also increases your chances of spotting something that looks worn or out of place before it becomes a more serious problem.

- **Clean and lubricate your drivetrain every 100 miles (160 km) or so:** a chain-cleaning device is one of the most effective ways to keep your chain in shape, but if you don't have one a basic method is to soak a clean rag with some degreaser and clasp the chain with it while you back-pedal with your other hand. Repeat until the rollers and side plates are clean. Don't forget to degrease your cassette, rear derailleur jockey wheels and crankset while you're at it – if these areas are still clogged with muck, they will simply spread more dirt as you're cleaning (and even more so when you get back on your bike and start cycling). Once everything is looking clean, rinse thoroughly with warm water and dry with a clean rag. Apply a drop of lubricant to the top of each chain link, again while back-pedalling with your hand, and wipe off the excess when you've finished to avoid it picking up dirt.

Note: If you don't know what terms like cassette, rear derailleur jockey wheels or crankset mean, check them out online – you will also find some helpful videos on YouTube on the whole cleaning/ degreasing process.

- **Look after your brakes:** check regularly that your pads are wearing evenly and, if they're not, sand them down until they're even and then ensure your brakes and wheel are properly centred to avoid it happening again (see 'One brake pad is dragging against the rim' in the next section for advice on how to do this). If the pads are wearing evenly, rough them up lightly with medium emery paper or sandpaper and give your wheel rims a thorough clean to improve 'grab' in any event. If you have disc brakes as opposed to rim brakes, detach the rear wheel and wipe down the rotor and discs with disc brake cleaner and a clean rag.

- **Keep your tyres properly inflated:** properly inflated tyres ride the bumps and absorb the shocks to give you a smooth ride. You will lose pressure on a ride, or even if your bike has just been waiting for you in the shed for a while, so always check your tyre pressures before setting off. As a rule of thumb, your tyre pressures should be in the following table's range, but you have to assess your individual need depending on your own weight and the surface you are going to be riding on (reduce by around 10 psi in the wet and when riding off-road on rougher surfaces). In any event, make sure you check the tyre manufacturer's guidance on the wall of your tyre for the recommended pressure range for your specific tyres.

| Road tyres | 80–130 psi |
|---|---|
| Mountain-bike tyres | 30–50 psi |
| Hybrid tyres | 50–70 psi |

### Get in touch with your inner bike

Whenever your ride feels a bit different or your bike makes an unfamiliar noise, bear in mind the following possibilities if it seems to be having an off day:

- **Creaking sound from one of the wheels:** a spoke may have loosened, so if you don't have a spoke wrench on you, tighten it with your fingers. Be sure to correct the tension properly when you have a chance, as riding on an unbalanced wheel is dangerous. If the tension of your spokes is uniform, the sound might be caused by a slight motion of the spokes against each other where they cross. If so, lightly lubricate the crossing point in question.

- **Creaking sound when you pedal:** tighten the bolts on the crankarms that your pedals are attached to. If the creaking continues, it may be coming from your bottom bracket. If you feel competent to do so, remove the crankarms, apply a trace of grease to the spindles and reinstall. Otherwise, or if that doesn't work, you should probably take your bike to a repair shop.

- **Pedalling causes loud skipping in certain gears:** there may be some debris between your cogs (or possibly even those on your bike). If you can see mud, grass, leaves, twigs or any other sort of foreign matter trapped in there, dig it out, because it might be preventing the chain from achieving a proper mesh on a particular cog. If there's no debris, a cog may be worn out and you may have to get the chain and cassette replaced.

- **Rear derailleur makes a constant squeaking noise:** the pulleys on your derailleur (the chain-management system that hangs below the cogs) may be dry and require lubrication on both sides.

- **Braking feels soft:** assuming the brake pads haven't worn down, the brake cable has probably stretched with use. Loosen the small brake-adjuster barrel and its associated lock ring (these will be found either on the brake caliper or next to the brake lever on the end of the handlebar). Now turn the barrel counterclockwise until the pads are close enough to the wheel rim to make the braking action feel tighter. Then screw the lock ring clockwise until it returns to its position on the cable housing. If your braking feels too hard, simply adjust the barrel in a clockwise direction to move the pads away from the wheel rim.

- **Braking feels 'grabby':** in all likelihood, you have a spot of damage to the wheel rim, which is hitting the brake pad at the same point in each wheel revolution. Take your bike to a mechanic.

- **One brake pad is dragging against the rim:** this is because it is closer to the rim than the pad on the other side, so turn your bike upside down and check the alignment of the wheel to see if it's out of true. If it is, take the bike to the repair shop. If the wheel looks centred but a pad still rubs, you need to re-centre the brake by turning a small adjustment screw (sometimes there are two, one on each side) found somewhere on the side or top of the brake caliper. Turn the screw or screws in small increments, until the two pads are equidistant from the rim.

- **Brakes squeal:** wipe the rim to remove any oil or cleaning residue. If that doesn't work, scuff the pads with sandpaper or a file. If that doesn't work, take your bike to a mechanic.

- **You hear a click with each pedal stroke:** one of the pedals has probably loosened, causing you to sit off-centre on the saddle. Tighten the offending pedal, remembering that the thread on the left-hand pedal runs in the opposite way to that on the right-hand pedal (this is to stop it unscrewing while you pedal). Just bear in mind that you always turn the pedal in question towards the front of the bike to loosen it and vice versa to tighten it.

- **Saddle creaks or clicks:** if it creaks, drip a tiny amount of oil around the rails where they enter the saddle, and into the clamp where it grips the rails (but bear in mind if you have a leather saddle that it's probably going to creak a bit anyway, because that's just a price you have to pay for being retro). If your saddle clicks, tighten the bolts that connect the saddle to the seat post.

# *IMPROVE YOUR CYCLING PERFORMANCE*

There are more books, manuals, web pages and YouTube videos than you can shake a spoke at on how to improve your confidence or performance on a bike, but here are some tips to get you going if you're new or just a bit rusty or forgetful.

### Cycle as much as you can

I know this is rather stating the obvious, but regularity and repetition really are key to achieving the fitness level you need to move up to the level of a competent cyclist. Many experts contend that you need to put in up to 12 months of hard, often painful graft in the saddle before it all clicks into place, from which point it becomes more of a joy than a slog. From that moment onwards you should have enough confidence in your own strength, stamina and riding ability to push yourself to your ever-increasing limits almost at will.

### Fix your foot to the pedal

Toe clips and straps and clip-in pedal systems are not essential, but many cyclists swear by the power and speed improvements they offer. They take a little bit of getting used to, but you'll very quickly get the hang of them.

They all help to create power through the full cycle of pedalling, not just in the pushing down phase. Pulling your pedals up behind you as much as you push down on them in front of you affords you an even spread of power and far more efficiency, which is especially helpful when climbing hills.

Bear in mind that clips and straps aren't much use in cities where you stop and start, though (if you stop at a traffic light and forget to unclip at least one of your feet, you will fall over).

## Climb more

One of the quickest and most effective ways to improve is to increase the amount of climbing you do. Going up hills of all lengths and gradients is a fantastic way to get fit at your own pace. Try repetitions of one hill or a longer hilly route and you'll soon notice a sharp increase in your strength and aerobic capacity.

Be sure to maintain a rhythm that's your own, though. If you're cycling with other people, don't try to match their cadence – it just won't work. Focus on your own legs and your own bike, on improving your own efficiency with your gears.

If you're feeling up to it, performing hill repetitions at the end of a ride will really build the strength in your legs and greatly increase the calories you burn. Find a hill that takes approximately 1–2 minutes to climb and use your gears to maintain a speed of roughly 80–90 rpm all the way to the top. Recover on the way back down and repeat three to five times.

As far as technique is concerned on the uphills, try to bear the following in mind:

- Keep your eye on the gradient ahead and feel for subtle changes in pedal resistance, as changing gear at exactly the right time will help you to maintain your momentum.

- Stay relaxed and hold the handlebar loosely – a tense body and/or a tight grip will make your job more difficult.

- Sit back on the seat and try not to favour one leg over the other.

- Stand up on your pedals from time to time in the style of Spanish rider Alberto Contador – not only can you exert more effort on the steeper sections in this way, you'll also enjoy the stretch and different muscles will take over to give your seat-climbing ones a short break.

- Concentrate on breathing all the way out as you exhale – your lungs will fill up of their own accord so you don't really need to bother too much about inhalation.

- Power over the crest of the hill just because you can.

## Cycle faster

The faster you cycle, the fitter you will become, and there are some surprisingly simple tweaks you can make to increase your speed:

- Pump up your tyres properly before every ride, as poorly inflated tyres are among the most common reasons for cyclists slowing down. Not only will your bike roll faster, you'll also be less likely to get punctures.

- Learn to control your braking technique, because using your brakes too often means having to pedal harder to regain speed, which interrupts your flow and slows you down. Whenever it's safe to do so, throw away the comfort blanket of your brakes and enjoy the liberating feeling of letting your bike just freewheel down slopes and round wide corners.

- Make yourself more aerodynamic: as wind resistance is the number one obstacle to speed, streamline your body as much as you can. Lose weight if you need to (a few weeks of regular cycling should do the trick) and lower your upper body when it's windy – sitting up straight in the wind will make you feel as if you just picked up a passenger. Positioning your pedals at quarter to and quarter past (i.e. horizontally) will also help to centre your weight and keep your riding position compact.

### How not to descend (unless you're Chris Froome)

Avoid at all costs the extreme descending position now adopted by Chris Froome and a few other top racers, whereby they sit on the top tube instead of the saddle, place their hands on the middle of the handlebar and extend their chin between their hands to rest on the stem. There's an even more aerodynamic descending pose called 'the Superman', which involves placing your belly on the saddle and projecting your legs off the back of the bike, but I'm not going to mention it here just in case you're daft enough to try it on a mountainside.

## Vary your effort

There is absolutely nothing wrong with cycling at the same pace, but varying your speed will get you fitter more quickly. Start with a steady 10-minute warm-up, then pedal hard for a mile or two at a pace that challenges you but remains manageable, then continue to alternate between the two tempos. Gradually increase your speed and distance at both speeds over time, but always remember to cool down with a 10-minute steady cycle at the end.

For even higher intensity, spend some sessions alternating between short, sharp bursts and equal recovery times, e.g. eyeballs out for 20 seconds, recover for 20 seconds, then repeat as often as you can until either your legs or your eyeballs can do no more. Even your commute can be turned into an interval workout by activating your bursts of speed between traffic lights or roundabouts, or so many lampposts, parked cars, trees or whatever else is available on your route to and from work (but only try this where it is absolutely safe to do so and keep your eyes on the traffic at all times).

### Cycling keeps you young

Research studies are forever telling us what we should eat and drink and how we should exercise, always with the promise of longer, healthier lives if we obey the latest rules. Cycling is no exception, with researchers at

King's College London and the University of Birmingham revealing how regular cycling can ward off the effects of ageing. Their study of 85 men and 41 women aged 55–79, all of whom cycled regularly, showed that on almost all measures of physical functioning and fitness, none of the cyclists showed their true age. One Dutch study of more than 30,000 people over a 15-year period even found that people who did not cycle to work were 39 per cent more likely to die at an earlier age than those who did.

## Understand your performance

Ever since sweat and snot gave way to pulse monitors and then strain gauges and power meters as the means of measuring performance on a bike, riders have enjoyed useful feedback on their live performance. Nowadays, that live feedback is followed by an impressive array of statistics and graphs to inform post-ride assessments.

Studying the analytics supplied by your system at the end of your ride will help you understand your performance within each of the segments of a particular ride (useful if the terrain was varied or if you included interval or tempo training during the ride) as well as your overall performance. It will show you how your average weighted power translates into speed and distance and the impact that increased power as you get fitter has on the latter two. You will then be able to understand and focus on your goals going forward, whether they entail bettering your own performance or that of others who are posting their performances alongside your own on the same system.

## Join a chain gang

Joining a pack of cyclists will help you to get faster and fitter while enjoying the sociable side of the sport. Pedalling along at the same speed within a like-minded group allows you to chat to each other in a way you couldn't if you were running, swimming or skydiving. For information about the many clubs that are available to cyclists of all ages, abilities and disciplines, see Chapter 5 ('In the Club').

## Exercise off the bike

Because your lower body does most of the work when you cycle, it's easy to forget the extent to which your core muscles keep you balanced and upright and how much strain you put on your arms and shoulders on a long ride, especially if your cycling is off-road. Poor core strength also means other muscles are over-engaged to compensate, which means you are more likely to rock from side to side. This unnecessary movement can bring on backache and saddle soreness. Here are some useful tips to ensure that your whole body gets the exercise it needs to support you on your bike rides:

- **Core**: include variations of the plank in your exercise routine, and check out windshield wipers, glute bridges and Russian twists while you're about it. Kettlebell swings are ideal for restoring your core and frame to its natural upright position off the bike, or try Pilates classes, which have a strong emphasis on core stability.

- **Arms and shoulders**: press-ups and triceps dips should form part of your upper-body routine. With a set of dumbbells you can add bicep curls, lateral raises and shoulder-press exercises.

- **Lower body**: leg exercises are ideal to strengthen your legs individually or collectively for the job. Lunges, hamstring curls and squats are great; single-leg hamstring curls and (if you have the balance) single-leg squats are even better.

- **All over**: a rowing machine at home or in the gym provides a great all-round exercise for cyclists, and hiking, running or swimming will keep you toned if you find yourself away from your bike for longer than you would like. Yoga is also ideal for keeping you flexible and for toning your muscles – and it's probably only fair you should treat them to some toning given all the hard work they do to keep you moving forward on your bike. For those familiar with yoga poses, the six essential ones for cyclists are the bridge, camel, cat-cow, pigeon, (reclining) hero and reclining bound angle (I assume the committee who give yoga poses cool names had a day off when the reclining bound angle cropped up for the first time).

### Keep your nutrition relevant

In the previous chapter, we looked at some of the nutrition requirements for racers and long-distance tourers, including those foodstuffs that aid recovery from serious injury. Here are some more general tips on nutrition for us cycling mortals.

- **Breakfast carbs**: bananas, peanut butter, Greek yoghurt, blueberries, oats, shredded wheat, mangoes, apples and sprouted bread are all ideal to increase your energy levels before a morning ride.

- **On-the-bike goodies**: energy drinks, gels and cereal bars come in many flavours, although many of those flavours bear a stronger resemblance to medicine than culinary treats. Glucose is good, but for longer distances make sure your drinks and gels also contain fructose, because the combination of the two sugars helps the absorption of carbohydrates. Caffeine is another useful ingredient in drinks and gels, especially towards the end of a longer ride. Jellied sweets and dried fruit are also good options for rides that last an hour or two.

- **Post-ride recovery**: we're talking protein here, so chicken, eggs, salmon, lentils, sweet potatoes, beetroot and rice are all good choices to help your muscles recover. If you didn't have time to prep anything before your ride, and don't have the time or energy to do it afterwards, chocolate milk or any protein shake will work as a substitute – and the even better news is that the shakes don't all taste like horse feed nowadays (although some still do).

- **Good at any time**: what's good for cyclists at any time is pretty much what's good for the other members of the human race at any time, including oily fish, lean meat, fruit and vegetables. Get maximum return from your five-a-day by including the nutrients supplied by watermelon, the healthy fats of an avocado, the potassium offered by bananas (and avocados) and the vitamins, minerals and antioxidants of tomatoes. A more enjoyable way for some of us to get antioxidants into our system is to have a couple of squares of dark chocolate every day.

- **Staying hydrated**: water remains the go-to form of daily hydration and we know all about the benefits of energy drinks during a ride. From a cycling point of view, water helps relieve cramps and sprains by keeping your joints lubricated and your muscles elastic. Alcohol won't hydrate you, but the odd beer or glass of wine won't do you much harm either – just remember that craft beer and organic wine have the nutrients and antioxidants of their base ingredients without the nasty chemicals used to protect the flavour and elongate the life of the regular stuff.

# CHAPTER 9

# *LOOKING THE PART*

*I'm not so sure about all the Lycra. I think the shorts and the
pointy helmets they wear during the time trial are really odd.*

Paul Smith, British fashion designer and mad-keen cyclist

Cycling apparel has come a long way since the early days of woollen jerseys
that weighed five times as much in the rain as they did in the sun, and the
leather skid-lids that passed for helmets in continental Europe for much of
the twentieth century. And female riders, no longer confined to the modest
knickerbockers of yesteryear, have the same choices that men have.

As far as raw material is concerned, progress came with the synthetics
that were popularised in the second half of the twentieth century, like rayon
and nylon and, for helmets, polystyrene. But even they seem antiquated in
the face of today's water-repellent, mesh-ventilated, moisture-transferring,
sun-protecting materials. In fact, clothing has become so sophisticated
that different apparel and different levels of protection are available for
different cycling sports. Take helmets: road racing demands a combination
of lightweight materials and reinforced protection from asphalt; mountain

bikers require robust, secure-fitting headgear with thick chinstraps to absorb the bumps and jars of rocky terrain; and BMX riders need motorbike-style full-face helmets with chin bar and drop-down visor, but very little in the way of ventilation (because their races last an average of 40 seconds).

### RE-CYCLED FACT

#### 'Catch!'

When UCI road-racing rules made the wearing of helmets compulsory in 2003, an exception was made for final summit climbs of more than 5 km (3.1 miles) in length. This resulted in the bizarre spectacle in that year's Tour de France of rider after rider throwing their helmets in the general direction of team helpers on l'Alpe d'Huez.

To see just how far we've come in the twenty-first century, let's have a look at some of the state-of-the-art clothing items that road-racing pros wear nowadays on board their state-of-the-art bikes:

**Helmet**: Aerodynamic, lightweight and breathable, today's carbon-fibre helmets have come a long way from the leather skullcaps and polystyrene shells of yesteryear. The Kask Bambino TT (time-trial) helmet is a fine example of today's state-of-the-art designs, being a sleek, black-and-silver

Buck Rogers-style affair with integrated visor attached by magnets, and as many air-intake and exhaust vents as you need to keep you cool on the road or track.

**Shoes**: Take the Bont Zero as an example: space-age design combined with space-age technology, these ergonomically shaped anti-stretch shoes weigh around 170 g (6 oz) each. Laminated fibreglass uppers nestle on top of a carbon monocoque chassis. If Carlsberg designed cycling shoes…

**Jersey**: Today's versions fit like an extra layer of skin to reduce friction and ensure an aerodynamic ride; developed to keep heat out and control moisture.

**Gloves**: Everything from superabsorbent to supergrip and superstretch to superventilated is available to the discerning pro rider, plus ergonomically positioned gel padding to distribute pressure evenly and absorb bumps, holes and cobbles.

**Legwear**: Cut for aggressive racing with scientifically designed padding. This is a very important clothing area for a rider, who is quite clearly never going to want his or her padding to be anything less than scientifically designed!

**Time-trial skinsuit**: Aerodynamic, wafer-thin, one-piece garment pretested in wind tunnels on the planet Jupiter. (I might have made up the bit about Jupiter, but you get my point.)

**Eyewear**: Lightweight, sweat-blocking, wraparound design and light-stabilising technology are matched only by the magnificence of the names that marketing types have come up with for these twenty-first-century accessories. How on earth is anyone supposed to choose between the Adidas Evil Eye Half Rim Pro and the Oakley Tour de France RadarLock? There are times when one pair of eyes simply isn't enough!

Back on planet earth, it is important to remember that perfectly ordinary clothing is fine for leisure-riding or short-distance commuting, providing that the clothing is not so loose fitting it could get caught up in a moving part. And never forget the option of pedal pushers, the most appropriately named item of clothing ever. Unless you live in a bike-friendly city like Amsterdam or Copenhagen, though, you might still want to consider a helmet if you're going into traffic.

If you do really want to look the part, however, you can spend several hundred pounds and beyond on top-of-the-range cycling gear from designer sportswear companies like Rapha. You can buy everything from base layers and arm warmers to wind jackets and African hair sheep leather gloves with military-level padding. Whether you consider this a bit unnecessary or not, you will be buying clothing that is likely to last you an awful lot of miles. You can also look out for special-edition clothing that commemorates this or that event, like the one-hundredth running of the

Giro d'Italia in 2017, and keep an eye on the growing cycle-wear collection of keen cyclist and fashion icon Paul Smith.

In recent years, the top designers have added a new dimension to their collections, as it is now possible to buy 'city clothing' that affords you the same breathable, moisture-control cycling that you've come to expect on your daily commute, but which still looks good enough to wear all day in the shops or workplace. Options include short cycling trench coats, organic-cotton stretch jeans and knitwear, shirts and bomber jackets that glow by night but not by day. There are even padded cycling underpants these days that look more suited to a date night than a training session.

# CHAPTER 10

# *FAMOUS EASY RIDERS*

*Nothing compares to the simple pleasure of a bike ride.*

John F. Kennedy, thirty-fifth president of the USA

This chapter looks at the myriad famous people who have fallen in love with the bicycle somewhere along the way, from writers and actors to pop stars, fashion designers and geniuses.

## *ENTREPRENEURS*

### Paul Smith

British fashion designer Paul Smith dreamt of racing professionally until a serious accident on his bike at the age of 16 put paid to his ambitions. Professional cycling's loss turned out to be the fashion world's gain, although he has managed to combine his two passions whenever the opportunity has arisen. He continues to produce a range of practical yet highly fashionable cycle-wear, and he is often commissioned to produce special-edition clothing or even bike designs to commemorate notable events. He worked with Derby bike manufacturer Mercian Cycles to design special-edition bikes that commemorated the company's sixtieth anniversary in 2006, and with Italian giant Pinarello to add a Paul Smith twist to their 2013 Dogma 65.1 Think 2 bikes. He was also commissioned to design the four leaders' jerseys for the 2013 Giro d'Italia.

## Alan Sugar

The British entrepreneur, and star of *The Apprentice*, took to cycling after a series of injuries forced him to give up his first sporting love, tennis. He regularly completes a 50-mile (80-km) loop around the Essex countryside on his top-of-the-range, custom-made Pinarello racing bike.

Other famous bike-riding entrepreneurs include:

- **Vivienne Westwood**: extrovert English fashion designer, who commutes to work on her Pashley.

- **Richard Branson**: in spite of a horrific bike accident in 2016 – in which his bike went over a cliff but fortunately he didn't – the Virgin boss remains a keen endurance cyclist. He has completed the 109.5-km (68-mile) Cape Argus tour in South Africa.

- **Clive Sinclair**: developer of the doomed C5 car and the lightweight A-bike, which folds down small enough to fit into a rucksack. An electric version of the A-bike was introduced in 2015.

## *MUSICIANS*

### John Lennon

'I must have been the happiest boy in Liverpool, if not the world,' John Lennon said of the time he was given his first bike after passing his 11-plus exam. It was a Raleigh Lenton Mk II and he loved it so much that he took it to bed with him that night. In later years, he was often photographed riding a bike, including with his fellow Beatles and with Yoko Ono. He even had a white bike to ride around the inside of the Hilton Hotel in Amsterdam when he was on honeymoon there with Yoko.

### Eric Clapton

Music aficionados may be familiar with the *Disraeli Gears* album that propelled the British band Cream (consisting of Eric Clapton, Ginger Baker and Jack Bruce) to 'supergroup' status in the late 1960s. Not all will be aware that the album title derived from a cycling malapropism. Eric Clapton was a former bike racer who had been forced to choose between the bike and the guitar, at least as far as his career was concerned. He was talking in the recording studio one day about the new racing bike he was thinking of buying when somebody asked him whether it had 'Disraeli gears' (meaning, of course, 'derailleur gears'). The album title was decided there and then.

### Madonna

The American pop superstar, actress and film director has often been spotted riding around London, New York and Malibu (i.e. near whichever of her homes she happened to be staying in at the time). She uses her bike to get to the gym or the recording studio as part of her overall fitness regime.

## David Byrne

The Scottish former Talking Heads front man does not own a car and is an active supporter of cycling, having used it as his main form of transport for most of his life, especially in his adopted city of New York. He has had a regular cycling column in *The New York Times* and has written elsewhere on the subject, including a 2009 book called *Bicycle Diaries*.

In 2008, he designed a series of bicycle parking racks in the style of the New York area they were to be placed in – such as a dollar sign for Wall Street and a coffee mug on Amsterdam Avenue near the Hungarian Pastry Shop.

Other famous bike-riding musicians include:

- **Beyoncé (Knowles-Carter)**: iconic American singer/songwriter/dancer/actress who says she rides to keep herself grounded.

- **Ian Brown**: English singer/songwriter and frontman with 1990s indie band The Stone Roses. He rode his bike slowly through the streets of London's Soho and Chinatown for the video for his solo single 'F.E.A.R.', which was then reversed to create the impression of him riding slowly backwards.

- **Tim Commerford**: bass player with American rock band Rage Against the Machine – they had to cancel a concert in 1995 after Commerford broke his wrist in a cycling accident.

- **Lily Allen**: English singer/songwriter who gave the Raleigh Chopper something of a comeback in the 2006 video for her 'LDN' single, and who is still spotted cycling around London on a regular basis.

- **Sting**: the English musician and singer/songwriter, and frontman with The Police, has been seen riding around his Tuscan vineyard estate with wife Trudie Styler.

- **Miley Cyrus**: the American singer, songwriter and actress is often seen cycling around LA on cool bikes, including her electric one.

## ACTORS
### Matt Damon
The American Hollywood actor is a keen cyclist and, in common with Richard Branson, has completed the 109.5-km (68-mile) Cape Argus event in South Africa on a tandem with his brother Kyle (the Cape Argus attracts more riders than any other sportive on the planet).

Other famous bike-riding actors include:

- **Brad Pitt** and **Angelina Jolie**: the American actors and film producers were often 'papped' cycling *en famille* around LA before they split up.

- **Hugh Jackman**: the Australian actor and producer had the wheels stolen from his bike during his film audition for *Les Misérables* – at least he got the part.

- **Gwyneth Paltrow**: the American actress, singer and food writer is a keen cyclist and was even married to a unicyclist – see Chris Martin below.

- **Pierce Brosnan**: the Irish actor, film producer and environmentalist with a licence to ride has often been spotted cycling around London and Malibu.

- **Jennifer Aniston**: the American actress worked as a bike messenger before hitting the big time as Rachel in *Friends* and remains a keen cyclist to this day.

### RE-CYCLED FACT

#### Tri-actors

It's no accident that actors Harrison Ford, Jennifer Lopez and Jon Hamm (of *Mad Men* fame) have looked good over the years, because they have all been known to compete in triathlons. The image seems well suited to the Indiana Jones character, and to J-Lo's booty-shaking routines, but not so much to the chain-smoking, whisky-drinking, womanising Don Draper. Never judge a 1960s ad-man by his cover.

## *TV PRESENTERS*
### Jeremy Clarkson

The TV presenter gets the award for Biggest Hypocrite on Two Wheels. Notwithstanding his public rants about the need to ban cyclists because they obstruct his beloved cars and don't even pay road tax, he has often been seen at weekends enjoying sneaky cycling trips with his wife.

Other famous bike-riding TV presenters (all of whom support the cycling cause and do much to raise money for charities with bike-related events) include:

- **Lorraine Kelly**: Scottish breakfast TV anchorwoman and cycling ambassador.

- **David Walliams**: English comedian, writer and actor, who completed a John O'Groats to Land's End (JOGLE) charity ride in 2010 despite a serious fall in the Lake District.

- **Phil Keoghan**: New Zealand-born TV presenter of American travel game show *The Amazing Race*.

- **Mike Tomalaris**: Australian TV's 'Mr Cycling' has covered the Tour de France since 1996.

- **Ryan van Duzer**: the US TV presenter has cycled across America and from Honduras to Colorado.

## *SCIENTISTS*
### Albert Einstein

When he wasn't being a genius, Einstein often relaxed by riding around on his bike. Even then, he didn't totally switch off, though, because he once said that he thought of the theory of relativity while out riding. He also compared life with riding a bike, saying that 'to keep your balance, you must keep moving'. As if we didn't already know that – it's not exactly rocket science, is it, Albert?

Other famous bike-riding scientists include:

- **David Attenborough**: the English broadcaster and second-to-none naturalist cycled well into his advancing years.

- **Stephen Hawking**: once a schoolboy and student like any other before developing motor neurone disease, the famous physicist loved to cycle and showed a particular talent for slow-bicycle races at St Albans School in Hertfordshire.

- **Bill Nye**: the American science educator and comedian, known as 'Bill Nye, the Science Guy', has been a keen cyclist all his life and has posted a wealth of fun tips online about how to buy and maintain the right bike for you and how best to ride it. He maintains that there is no more efficient machine than a human being on a bike: 'Thirty miles on a bowl of oatmeal; you can't come close to that,' he says.

# WRITERS

## Mark Twain

Mark Twain learnt to ride on a penny-farthing in the early 1880s. It did not come easily to him, and he penned a typically hilarious account of the experience in his essay *Taming the Bicycle*. In this, he describes how he managed to hospitalise his instructor by constantly landing on top of him, and how he managed to perfect the 'voluntary dismount', but only long after he had perfected the involuntary version. He concludes the essay with the following advice to his readers: 'Get a bicycle. You will not regret it, if you live.'

Other famous bike-riding writers include:

- **Arthur Conan Doyle**: there is photographic evidence of the British author out and about on his bike, and he included the 1903 short story *The Adventure of the Solitary Cyclist* in his Sherlock Holmes series.

- **Ernest Hemingway**: the American writer and journalist was a keen cyclist and an avid follower of European road racing between the world wars.

- **Leo Tolstoy**: the Russian writer learnt to ride at the ripe old age of 67 (see also next chapter).

- **Thomas Hardy**: the English novelist and poet claimed that he loved to ride to avoid contact with other human beings.

- **Sylvia Plath**: the American novelist and poet imported her own bike when she went to study at Cambridge in 1950s England.

- **H. G. Wells**: the English writer was photographed tandem riding with his wife and indulged his love of cycling in an 1896 novel about a cycling holiday, *The Wheels of Chance*.

- **Philip Larkin**: the bald, bespectacled and bicycle-clipped English poet and novelist loved to visit churches on his bike, and may even have come across a few Whitsun weddings while he was about it.

- **Virginia Woolf**: the English writer travelled far and wide across the Sussex countryside as a teenager by combining rail and bicycle travel.

## SPORTSMEN AND WOMEN

### Jenson Button

Cycling formed an integral part of the English Formula One driver's training regime. He regularly tested his fitness on the infamous 12-km (7.5-mile) Col de la Madone ('Madonna climb') near Menton on the French Riviera, and therefore not far from his home in Monte Carlo.

### Zara Tindall

The top equestrian and granddaughter of Queen Elizabeth II may be more comfortable on a horse, but she has proved pretty handy on a bike as well on the occasions she has turned out to play bicycle polo for charity. She has even managed to rope her cousins Prince William and Prince Harry into her team.

## Lawrence Dallaglio and Andrew 'Freddie' Flintoff

The English rugby and cricket sporting legends raised over £2 million for charity when they spearheaded a team of 15 riders across an epic 1,728-mile (2,782-km) challenge over 22 days from Olympia in Greece (the home of the Olympics) to London in 2012.

Other famous bike-riding sportsmen and women include:

- **David Beckham**: the former England footballer who won league titles in four different countries was often snapped out riding with his sons in LA.

- **Tiger Woods**: the American golfer starts most days with a run or a bike ride as part of his strict physical training regime.

- **Fernando Alonso**: the Spanish Formula One driver rides his bike at close to professional pace.

- **Abby Wambach**: the former American women's soccer player loved to mountain bike when she wasn't busy scoring goals for the USA.

- **Geoff Hurst**: the English hat-trick hero of the 1966 World Cup football final has often ridden for charitable causes.

## POLITICIANS AND ROYALS

### Boris Johnson

As London's high-profile mayor, Johnson pushed hard for more, safer cycling lanes in the UK's capital. He famously scrapped the 'bendy buses' because of concerns that cyclists might get trapped on the inside as the buses negotiated their way around corners.

### Crown Prince Frederik and Crown Princess Mary of Denmark

The Crown Prince and his Australian-born wife cycle regularly in and around the palace grounds and think nothing of ferrying their young children to school in a cargo bike.

Other famous bike-riding politicians and royals include:

- **John F. Kennedy**: the thirty-fifth president of the USA famously said that nothing compared to the simple pleasures of a bike ride (although I can't help thinking that spending time with Marilyn Monroe must have been a pretty close second).

- **Barack Obama**: the forty-fourth president of the USA was often photographed out riding with his family or with celebrity 'mates' like Brad Pitt.

- **Queen Beatrix of the Netherlands**: there is even a life-size bronze statue of her riding her bike, but she will have more time for the real thing in any event since she abdicated the throne in 2013.

- **David Cameron**: the British prime minister famously had his bike stolen while he picked up a few bits of salad in his local Tesco in West London.

- **Arnold Schwarzenegger**: the Austrian-American actor and former governor of California was often snapped riding 'stateside' and took to the London streets on a Barclays 'Boris' bike in 2012 with the London mayor himself.

---

### Tour de Trump

Donald Trump, the forty-fifth president of the USA, staged the Tour de Trump road race in the USA in 1989 and 1990, claiming that it would one day be as prestigious as the Tour de France. In 2015, he promised never to enter a bike race while president, after criticising Secretary of State John Kerry for falling off his bike and breaking his leg in the French Alps during a break from nuclear disarmament talks with Iran in neighbouring Switzerland. This is all very disappointing, because now the world will never know how many cyclists who started out in a race with Trump would be there at the end. Just his family members would be my guess.

---

## FAMOUS UNICYCLISTS
### Chris Martin

If evidence were required that the Coldplay singer/songwriter and instrumentalist could ride a unicycle, it can be found in the band's video for their 2011 'Paradise' single, when he unicycled on the South African plains in an elephant's costume (as you do).

### Mark Owen, Jason Orange and Howard Donald

The (current and former) Take That members learnt to unicycle for their 2009 *The Circus* tour, bringing the house down whenever they unicycled on to the stage, only to be outdone by Gary Barlow following behind on a miniature clown's bike.

### Eddie Izzard

As he proved in a 1998 episode of hit Channel 4 show *TFI Friday*, the British comedian and actor Eddie Izzard can do more than just unicycle – he can escape from the 'Manacles of Death' within 10 seconds while riding a unicycle!

### Michael Crawford

The English actor/singer learnt to unicycle, juggle, walk a tightrope, trampoline and walk on stilts for his lead role in the 1980s hit stage musical *Barnum*, based on the life of the eponymous circus showman.

Other famous unicyclists include:

- **Rupert Grint**: the English actor who played Ron Weasley in the *Harry Potter* films often works a different kind of magic on his unicycle.

- **Donald Rumsfeld**: it is pretty much an unknown known that the former US Secretary of Defense was a capable unicyclist.

- **Formula One drivers**: F1 drivers past and present who have swapped four wheels for one to keep themselves entertained in between races include Mika Häkkinen, Lewis Hamilton and Nico Rosberg.

# CHAPTER 11

# *STRANGE BICYCLE FACTS*

*A bicycle ride around the world begins with a single pedal stroke.*

Scott Stoll, American round-the-world cyclist

As you might expect from something that has had a huge influence on the cultures of the world for more than 150 years now, bicycles have been the cause of some very strange customs and habits and have led to some extreme versions of the pastime. They have also found their way into our music, literature and art. This chapter provides some lesser-known facts about how the bicycle has affected our lives across successive generations.

## 'DR STANLEY, I PRESUME?'

British-American Tom Stevens was the first person to circle the globe by bicycle, and he did so on a penny-farthing between April 1884 and December 1886. He started off by crossing the plains and mountains of America from San Francisco to Boston, astonishing cowboys and Indians alike as he went.

Having sailed east to Liverpool, he cycled through Berkhamsted, the town of his birth, before taking the Newhaven–Dieppe ferry to continental Europe. He later rested in Constantinople before taking in Mesopotamia (present-day Iraq) and Persia (present-day Iran), where he saw out a winter as a guest of the Shah. Afghanistan, India, China and Japan followed.

A couple of years following his circumnavigation, this remarkable man led a successful East African expedition to find Henry Morton Stanley, the explorer who had found David Livingstone and then wandered 'off map' himself. Between them, they must have had some stories to tell around the campfire.

## WHAT'S IN A NAME?

A bicycle was not always called a bicycle. Much more descriptive names like 'pedestrian-accelerator', 'dandy-charger' and 'hobby horse' had their chance, but they blew it (and things were to go from bad to worse for the hobby horse, as it later sank to the ignominious depths of pantomime and morris dancing). In the end, Victorian Britain decided to throw its lot in with its French (*bicyclette*) and Italian (*bicicletta*) cousins in opting for a Latin-Greek combo, 'bi' being Latin for 'two' and 'kyklos' being Greek for 'circle'. And that's how we all came to be riding 'two-circles'.

## TREAD CAREFULLY, MY DEAR WATSON

Arthur Conan Doyle was a keen solo cyclist and was also photographed on a high-wheel tandem tricycle with Mrs Doyle (probably his first wife, Louisa). It was only natural, then, that he should imbue Sherlock Holmes with superlative bicycle-tread-spotting abilities. As Sherlock declared in *The Adventure of the Priory School*, 'I am familiar with forty-two different impressions left by tyres.' On the particular tyre impression in question, he further explained to a confused Watson: 'This track, as you perceive, was made by a rider who was going from the direction of the school.'

## BUGLE BOYS

The early riding clubs were rather stuffy affairs, with captains appointed to maintain discipline on the road, and members expected to wear their badged uniforms at all times, especially when out riding. Potholes were the natural enemy of the penny-farthing in particular, and so each club had a bugle boy up front to sound the alarm whenever he came across a hole or rut (which was often).

## BEST-KNOWN SONG ABOUT A BIKE

Mungo Jerry ('Push Bike Song'), Hawkwind ('Silver Machine') and Katie Melua ('Nine Million Bicycles') are strong contenders for having produced the best-known bike song ever, but the award must surely go to Queen's 1978 'Bicycle Race'. The original video, which was edited or banned in many countries, included a stadium bike race involving only naked girls, and the musical bridge included a section of said naked ladies simultaneously ringing their bicycle bells. All together now: 'I want to ride my bicycle...'

## MOST PAINFUL JOKE ABOUT A BIKE

*Truth hurts. Maybe not as much as jumping on a bicycle with the seat missing, but it hurts.*

Lieutenant Frank Drebin (Leslie Nielsen), *The Naked Gun 2½: The Smell of Fear*

## ROUND-THE-WORLD RECORDS

In 2012, Yorkshireman Mike Hall smashed the round-the-world cycling record by 14 days, taking just 92 days to cover around 18,000 miles (28,800 km), which was an average of around 200 miles (320 km) a day. The physical obstacles he had to overcome on his trip included a huge grizzly bear in New Jersey and a lot of roadkill in India (flattened snakes a speciality).

In 2017, Scottish adventurer Mark Beaumont smashed Hall's record by a further 13 days, having taken 78 days 14 hours 40 minutes to complete his 'Around the World in Eighty Days' challenge for charity. Riding from 4 a.m. to 10 p.m., he covered 240 miles (386 km) and consumed 9,000 calories – mostly while riding – each day. During the trip, he lost 13 lb (5.9 kg) of muscle, broke his arm and smashed a front tooth.

## THE BT MILLION POUND BIKE RIDE

In 2010, seven celebrities raised over £1 million for the Sport Relief charity when they cycled in shifts from John O'Groats to Land's End in four days. TV presenters Davina McCall and Fearne Cotton joined comedians David Walliams, Jimmy Carr, Miranda Hart, Russell Howard and Patrick Kielty to endure sub-zero temperatures, blizzards, cuts, bruises and saddle sores to achieve their mission. I hope someone had the decency to run them a nice, hot bath when they got to the finish.

## COUNT LEARNER TOLSTOY

As we have seen, the many great writers who have used bike-riding as a form of relaxation away from the writing desk include Ernest Hemingway, Thomas Hardy, Sylvia Plath, H. G. Wells, Philip Larkin, Virginia Woolf, Leo Tolstoy and Arthur Conan Doyle. None of the others, however, were as old as Tolstoy when they learnt to ride. He was 67 when, in 1895, the Moscow Society of Velocipede-Lovers provided him with a free bike and instruction, in the hope that this would help him get over the death of his youngest (and thirteenth) child.

## THE ART OF CYCLING

Salvador Dalí's affection for cycling is reflected in a number of his paintings, in some of which a horde of bearded cyclists ride in various directions with different objects on their heads: round stones in *Illumined Pleasures* (1929); long loaves of bread in *Babaouo* (1932); and heavy stones that hold down the ends of a wedding veil as the bikes are ridden by deathly figures past a grand piano in *Sentimental Conversation* (1944).

## DROOPY CHAPS AND FRISKY GALS

Saddles have always been a cause for concern for people who ride bikes over long periods, and were a particular concern for those early riders who cycled over potholes, ruts and cobblestones. The threat to male sexual performance and productivity was seen as very real, and resulted in the trial of many different saddle sizes and materials. It also spawned the groin-protecting 'bike jockey strap', or 'jockstrap'.

Victorian society quickly concluded that the problem for women, however, was quite the opposite of impotence, and manufacturers sought solutions to the otherwise inevitable state of permanent arousal in the female bike rider. Saddles were split in two to ensure that ladies rested on their sitting bones as opposed to their, er, non-sitting bits.

## A LITTLE CORNER OF ITALY

Cycling is popular in many African countries owing to the influence of their one-time Italian and French colonial rulers. This is especially true in the former Italian colony of Eritrea, in East Africa, where road cycling is the national sport. Eritrean riders have dominated the African Cycling Championships (in road and time-trial events) for several years. In the capital, Asmara, there are said to be more pizzerias, ice-cream parlours and cappuccino-serving coffee bars per square metre than anywhere else outside of Italy.

## MOST SOUTHERLY BIKE RIDE

Captain Thomas Orde-Lees of the Royal Marines was a member of Ernest Shackleton's 1914–1917 Imperial Trans-Antarctic Expedition. When the *Endurance* got stuck in pack ice, Shackleton encouraged activities among the men to keep morale up. Orde-Lees, a fitness fanatic, had taken his bike with him on the expedition and took every opportunity to ride it on the pack ice. Nine months on, the *Endurance* got crushed by the shifting ice and broke up.

They survived the next six months on the original ship's provisions and on what they could hunt as they hauled their lifeboats over the ice. After they were finally able to launch the lifeboats off the end of the icepack, they reached the dry land of Elephant Island, from where Shackleton and a few others set off on a perilous lifeboat journey to seek help 800 miles (1,300 km) away on South Georgia. Those left behind, including Orde-Lees, somehow survived a further five months, using two overturned lifeboats as their homes. They were eventually rescued by Shackleton and, quite miraculously, everyone on the expedition survived, although Orde-Lees did have to abandon his bike.

## MOST PEOPLE ON A BIKE RIDE

On New Year's Eve 2011, tens of thousands of Taiwanese took to their bikes simultaneously to establish a world record for the number of participants in a mass bike ride. One local news source put the figure at 72,919; another put it at 114,606. Either way, it was an appropriate record for a country that houses Giant, the largest bike-manufacturing company in the world.

## MOST BANNED SUBSTANCES

In 2012, French amateur rider Alexandre Dougnier was banned after a urine sample revealed a total of 12 illegal substances, thought to be a record for a single sample.

## LONGEST RIDE GOING NOWHERE

In 2010, 52-year-old American George Hood set the world record for the longest time riding a stationary bike: 222 hours, 22 minutes, 22 seconds. As he was allowed a 5-minute break for every hour he was in the saddle, it took him ten days. By way of comparison, it takes around 92 hours to ride the Tour de France over three weeks, with two rest days and a good night's sleep in between stages.

## NEVER MIND THE BUZZCOCKS

The Tour de France theme tune made popular by British television coverage of the race, and now the sound of a million mobile phone ringtones each summer, was composed by Pete Shelley of punk rock band Buzzcocks fame.

## GUINNESS WORLD RECORDS

The official Guinness World Records lists over 50 results in the cycling category. Here is my top ten:

1. Farthest distance cycled in a year (86,573 miles/139,326 km) – by American Amanda Coker in 2017.

2. World hour record (33.88 miles/54.53 km) – by Englishman Bradley Wiggins in 2015.

3. Longest distance cycling backwards on a unicycle (68 miles/109.44 km) – by American Steve Gordon in 1999.

4. Highest bunny hop over a static bar on a bicycle (4 ft 8 in./1.42 metres) – by Spaniard Benito Ros in 2009.

5. Fastest downhill speed on a bicycle on snow or ice (138 mph/222 km/h) – by Frenchman Eric Barone at Les Arcs in 2000.

6. Farthest distance cycled underwater (4.16 miles/6.7 km) – by German Jens Stötzner in 2013.

7. Longest distance cycled in 1 hour with no hands (23.25 miles/37.4 km) – by American Erik Skramstad over 62 laps of the Las Vegas Speedway track in 2009.

8. Most vertical metres cycled in 24 hours (20,050 metres/65,780 feet) – achieved simultaneously by Austrian twins Horst and Gernot Turnowsky in the Austrian Alps in 2007.

9. First trick cycling 'loop the loop' (1904) – by an Ancillotti troupe member at the Barnum & Bailey Circus.

10. Most consecutive artistic cycling rounds in the raiser head tube reverse/shoulder stand position (four) – by German sisters Carla and Henriette Hochdorfer in 2010. I don't know what this means but it sounds mighty impressive!

## ANNIE 'LONDONDERRY'

Latvian-born American Annie Kopchovsky was the first woman to cycle round the world, travelling only with a change of clothing and a pearl-handled revolver. The Londonderry Lithia Spring Water Company paid her to carry its placard on her bike and to adopt their name as her own. Setting off alone from Boston in 1894, at the age of 24 and already a mother of three children, she took nine months to cycle through parts of France, Egypt, Jerusalem, modern-day Yemen, Sri Lanka and Singapore. Arriving back in San Francisco, she took another six months to cycle the length and breadth of America before finally returning to Boston.

## DOGGONE!

Dogs were more than just a nuisance to the early cyclists, especially those cyclists who were atop high-wheelers like the penny-farthing, who could easily be toppled by the wee, jumping, barking beasts. Victorian cyclists in Britain carried small-calibre pistols to take care of the problem (remember, this was back in the days before dogs were afforded the same status in society as human children); American riders carried ammonia sprays; and German riders went the whole hog with gunpowder-filled anti-dog grenades.

## CAN'T BEAT THE REAL THING...

The Uzbek sprinter Djamolidine Abdoujaparov terrified TV commentators with his nine syllables and fellow riders with his erratic, flailing riding style. Things came to a head in 1991, on the final Tour de France sprint on the Champs-Élysées. The 'Tashkent Terror', as he was unaffectionately known, swerved into an oversized cardboard Coke can on the barriers and came off his bike with sufficient force to break his collarbone, on top of numerous other minor injuries and concussion. He eventually limped the

100 metres to the finishing line before being taken to hospital, because it was a requirement to finish the race in order to win the Tour's green jersey competition. Because he was in hospital at the time, he is the only winner of a Tour competition to miss the presentation of his own prize on the Champs-Élysées.

## DAREDEVIL RIDER

The most famous of all the Niagara daredevils, 'The Great Blondin' (real name Jean François Gravelet) crossed Niagara Falls on a tightrope several times in the second half of the nineteenth century. On one occasion, he delighted the watching crowds by doing so on a bicycle. On other occasions he walked it blindfold, or on stilts, or pushing a wheelbarrow or with his manager on his back.

## EXTREME BIKING

Extreme biking has taken many forms, including cycling along shark-infested seabeds, riding out to the edge of a precipice over the Grand Canyon, leaping gorges, riding along unprotected cliff edges, freefall parachuting (with your bike to break the landing) and frightening downhill descents like the infamous Repack in Fairfax, California. I have set a target of how many of those amazing feats I would like to achieve in my lifetime. None.

## BIKES ON FILM

Bicycles have often been featured on our movie screens, and not just as props. From cameo appearances to starring roles, and sometimes even as the subject of the film itself, here are my top ten classic bike moments captured for your viewing pleasure:

### 1. *The Wizard of Oz* (1939)

The scene where the evil Miss Almira Gulch rides her classic step-through roadster away from the farm with Dorothy's pet dog, Toto, in the basket had audiences everywhere screaming 'monster!' The frightening music from that scene enjoyed a resurgence in recent years as a popular mobile phone ringtone known as 'Wicked Witch of the West'.

### 2. *Ladri di Biciclette (Bicycle Thieves)* (1948)

Consistently lauded as one of the great films of world cinema, it follows the plight of a father in post-war Italy as he struggles to recover his stolen bike, without which he cannot get the work he needs to feed his family. Bike scenes abound but we are denied a happy ending, as the stolen bike in question is never recovered.

### 3. *The Sound of Music* (1965)

'Do-Re-Mi' on a bike! Well, on eight bikes, actually. Does cinema get more iconic than a Rodgers and Hammerstein classic being belted out by Julie Andrews and seven Alpine children on roadsters?

### 4. *Butch Cassidy and the Sundance Kid* (1969)

Who could forget that idyllic bike scene as the boys took some time out on a farm in between robberies? The bowler-hatted Butch (Paul Newman) took

Etta Place (Katharine Ross) for a spin on the handlebar of his 'safety' bike as B. J. Thomas sang 'Raindrops Keep Fallin' on My Head' to complete the perfect movie moment.

### 5. *A Day Out* (1972)
Playwright and keen cyclist Alan Bennett's first televised play was this half-hour short film about a Yorkshire cycling club on their outing from Halifax to Fountains Abbey in the summer of 1911. Studley Royal and Ripon are among the locations as we are transported back to simpler times. The tandem crash actually happened and filming had to be edited around the ensuing hospital visit for the two cast members involved.

### 6. *Breaking Away* (1979)
Winner of an Oscar, a Golden Globe and a BAFTA, this coming-of-age comedy drama about four American college graduates revolves around the passion one of them has for road racing. There are some great racing scenes when a professional Italian road-racing team comes to town, and during the recreation of the 'Little 500', an annual bike race held at Indiana University.

### 7. *E.T. the Extra-Terrestrial* (1982)
BMX bikes hadn't been around for long when they landed their first starring film role – and what a role it was. In the 1982 Spielberg classic, the cute extra-terrestrial took his young friend Elliott flying across the night sky, and the flying BMX against the full moon remains one of the most iconic images in movie history.

### 8. *BMX Bandits* (1983)

Nicole Kidman starred as the crime-fighting, BMX-riding teenager in the Australian children's adventure film *BMX Bandits*. Right from the opening scenes alongside the waterfronts of Manly, and later against the backdrop of Sydney, the film highlights time and again the off-road versatility of the BMX at a time when the BMX craze was sweeping the planet.

### 9. *Fight Club* (1999)

There is a scene in *Fight Club* where Tyler Durden (Brad Pitt) is cycling through the rooms of the house the two main protagonists share and goes head first over the handlebar. This initially happened as an accident when the cameras weren't rolling, but the crew and actors found it so funny that they then recreated it for the film. The first rule of Cycling Club is that you have to watch where you're going, Brad.

### 10. *Transporter 3* (2008)

The 'Best Use of a BMX Ever' award must surely go to Frank Martin (Jason Statham) in the third instalment of the French car-action trilogy. Having been carjacked while taking a phone call, he commandeers the nearest form of transport, a BMX bike, and sets off in hot pursuit. Having caught up with the top-of-the-range Audi on the 'borrowed' BMX (of course he does), Frank then does what Frank does best – feet first through the car window, he boots the carjacker straight out the passenger-side door while he himself lands safely in his usual driving-seat position. Perhaps even cooler than flying past the moon with an alien in your front basket? You decide.

# CHAPTER 12

# *CONTINUING THE REVOLUTION*

I hope you have enjoyed my miscellaneous ramblings about all things bike and that you feel inspired to do more of whatever it is you want to do on whatever size and shape of bike that is suited to your needs.

The great news for us all is that, after the ups and downs of the past hundred years or so, cycling has done more than just survive into the twenty-first century – it has flourished all over again. The sport of road racing in particular has gone global. Bike technology continues to develop at an impressive pace, and sales of bikes are on a distinctly upward trend. The cycling infrastructure in town and country is improving all the time. It has taken a while, but cycling has without doubt become popular again.

It doesn't matter how you ride, just ride. Do it for fun, to stay fit and healthy, to clear your head, to feed your need for speed or to satisfy your competitive urges. Or all of the above. I leave you with the profound words of the great Eddy Merckx when asked what advice he might give to other riders:

Ride lots.

# ACKNOWLEDGEMENTS

My thanks to Summersdale Publishers for the opportunity to refresh this book four years on from its original publication as *The Joy of Cycling*, in particular to Robert Drew for his expert project management and editing, and Chris Turton for his always sound technical input on all things bike. Thanks also to Stephanie Smith for tidying the book up nicely with a thoroughly professional copy-edit, and to the eagle-eyed Derek Donnelly for his impressive attention to detail in the final proofread.

## OTHER BOOKS BY RAY HAMILTON
## (ALL PUBLISHED BY SUMMERSDALE)

*For the Love of the Army* (2017)

*For the Love of the Navy* (2017)

*A Short History of Britain in Infographics* (2017)

*Knowledge: Stuff You Ought to Know* (2016)

*M25: A Circular Tour of the London Orbital* (2015)

*Trains: A Miscellany* (2015)

*The Joy of Golf* (2014)

*The Joy of Cycling* (2013)

*Le Tour de France: The Greatest Race in Cycling History* (2013)

*Military Quotations: Stirring Words of War and Peace* (2012)

ANNA HUGHES

# PEDAL
# POWER

## INSPIRATIONAL STORIES FROM
## THE WORLD OF CYCLING

# PEDAL POWER

Anna Hughes

ISBN: 978-1-78685-006-5

£9.99

A bike can be so many different things – a simple way of navigating busy city streets or enjoying quiet lanes, a cross-country steed to take a rider up hill and down dale or even a world-beating racing machine. What unites everyone who rides is that they each have their own cycling story to tell.

This book collects inspirational stories from riders around the world, both ordinary and extraordinary, from the cyclist who conquered Mont Ventoux on a Boris bike, to the trials rider who hops from building to building, to classic tales of Grand Tour rivalries and legendary cycling records of days gone by. Essential reading for anyone who loves life on two wheels.

# SPAIN TO NORWAY

## ON A BIKE CALLED

## REGGIE

ANDREW P. SYKES

# SPAIN TO NORWAY ON A BIKE CALLED REGGIE

Andrew P. Sykes

ISBN: 978-1-84953-990-6

£9.99

## MEET ANDREW: FRENCH TEACHER, WRITER AND LONG-DISTANCE CYCLIST.

## NOW, MEET REGGIE, HIS BIKE.

With two European cycling adventures already under his belt, Andrew was ready for a new challenge. Exchanging his job as a teacher in Oxfordshire for an expedition on Reggie the bike, he set off on his most daring trip yet: a journey from Tarifa in Spain to Nordkapp in Norway – from Europe's geographical south to its northernmost point. Join the duo as they take on an epic ride across nearly 8,000 km of Europe, through mountains, valleys, forests and the open road, proving that no matter where you're headed, life on two wheels is full of surprises.

If you're interested in finding out more about our books,
find us on Facebook at **Summersdale Publishers** and
follow us on Twitter at **@Summersdale**.

# www.summersdale.com

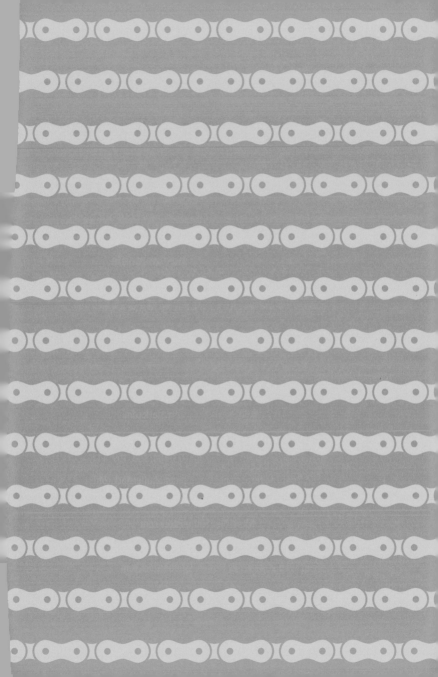

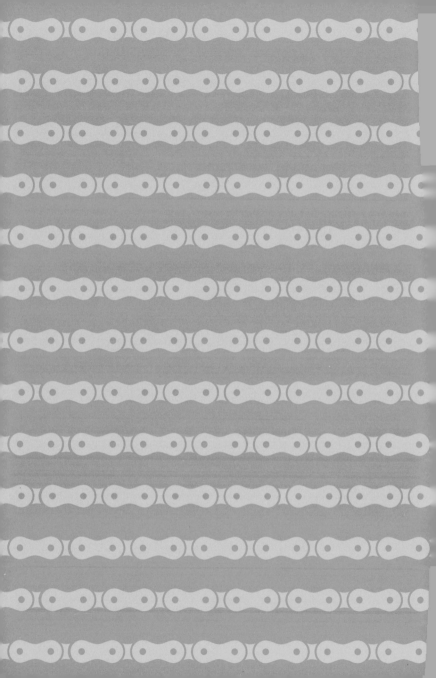